ROUTLEDGE LIBRARY EDITIONS:
LIBRARY AND INFORMATION SCIENCE

Volume 13

BUDGETS FOR ACQUISITIONS

BUDGETS FOR ACQUISITIONS
Strategies for Serials, Monographs, and Electronic Formats

Edited by
SUL H. LEE

LONDON AND NEW YORK

First published in 1991 by The Haworth Press, Inc.

This edition first published in 2020
by Routledge
2 Park Square, Milton Park, Abingdon, Oxon OX14 4RN

and by Routledge
52 Vanderbilt Avenue, New York, NY 10017

Routledge is an imprint of the Taylor & Francis Group, an informa business

© 1991 The Haworth Press, Inc.

All rights reserved. No part of this book may be reprinted or reproduced or utilised in any form or by any electronic, mechanical, or other means, now known or hereafter invented, including photocopying and recording, or in any information storage or retrieval system, without permission in writing from the publishers.

Trademark notice: Product or corporate names may be trademarks or registered trademarks, and are used only for identification and explanation without intent to infringe.

British Library Cataloguing in Publication Data
A catalogue record for this book is available from the British Library

ISBN: 978-0-367-34616-4 (Set)
ISBN: 978-0-429-34352-0 (Set) (ebk)
ISBN: 978-0-367-40961-6 (Volume 13) (hbk)
ISBN: 978-0-367-40973-9 (Volume 13) (pbk)
ISBN: 978-0-367-81023-8 (Volume 13) (ebk)

Publisher's Note
The publisher has gone to great lengths to ensure the quality of this reprint but points out that some imperfections in the original copies may be apparent.

Disclaimer
The publisher has made every effort to trace copyright holders and would welcome correspondence from those they have been unable to trace.

Budgets for Acquisitions: Strategies for Serials, Monographs, and Electronic Formats

Sul H. Lee
Editor

The Haworth Press
New York • London • Sydney

Budgets for Acquisitions: Strategies for Serials, Monographs, and Electronic Formats has also been published as *Journal of Library Administration*, Volume 14, Number 3 1991.

© 1991 by The Haworth Press, Inc. All rights reserved. No part of this work may be reproduced or utilized in any form or by any means, electronic or mechanical, including photocopying, microfilm and recording, or by any information storage and retrieval system, without permission in writing from the publisher. Printed in the United States of America.

The Haworth Press, Inc. 10 Alice Street, Binghamton, NY 13904-1580
EUROSPAN/Haworth, 3 Henrietta Street, London WC2E 8LU England
ASTAM/Haworth, 162-168 Parramatta Road, Stanmore, Sydney, N.S.W. 2048 Australia

Library of Congress Cataloging-in-Publication Data

Budgets for Acquisitions: strategies for serials, monographs, and electronic formats/ Sul H. Lee, editor.
    p. cm.
    "Has also been published as Journal of library administration, volume 14, number 3, 1991" – T.p. verso.
    ISBN 1-56024-158-6 (acid-free paper)
    1. Acquisitions (Libraries) – Costs. 2. Library materials – Prices. 3. Program budgeting. 4. Library finance. I. Lee, Sul H.
Z689.A243 1991
025.2 '1 – dc20   91-12603
                                                                                                                    CIP

Budgets for Acquisitions: Strategies for Serials, Monographs, and Electronic Formats

CONTENTS

Budgeting for Monographs, Serials, and Electronic
   Databases—How Should the Tart Be Cut?   1
      Roger K. Hanson

The Challenge of Maintaining Research Collections
   in the 1990s   17
      Jeffrey Gardner

Monograph Collections in Scientific Libraries: Sacrificial
   Lambs in the Library Lea?   27
      Daniel T. Richards

Been Down So Long, It Looks Like Up to Me   49
      Dana Alessi

The Electronic Library: Analysis and Decentralization
   in Collection Decisions   71
      Malcolm Getz

J & B the Proper Blend: Harsh Reality or Seamless System   85
      Charles Hamaker

Who Gets What: Allocating the Library's Materials Budget   99
      Robert L. Houbeck, Jr.

Balancing Collections, Balancing Budgets in Academic
   Libraries   121
      Carolyn Bucknall

Introduction

During the past five years the University of Oklahoma Libraries and the University of Oklahoma Foundation have jointly sponsored conferences focusing on the impact of rising costs on library budgets and management. The papers presented in this volume were originally presented at the 1990 conference, "Acquisitions Budgets: Strategies for Serials, Monographs, and Electronic Formats." This conference investigated the many issues involved in acquiring information in the different formats currently available.

Eight papers were presented by librarians, higher education adminstrators and vendors. The topics covered by the authors offer an examination of many important issues facing librarians. Roger Hanson, Director of Libraries at the University of Utah, provides an overview of many of the problems facing academic libraries through a discussion of his personal experiences. Jeffrey Gardner, Executive Director of the Association of Research Libraries, outlines some of the issues facing research libraries with particular attention to the advent of electronic formats and networking and possible strategies for the future. Daniel Richards, Collection Development Officer for the National Library of Medicine, focuses on the cost trends for collections in scientific libraries. The paper analyzes a ten-year period of data and the results of a survey about changing collection development patterns in scientiric libraries. Dana Alessi, Director of Academic marketing for Baker & Taylor discusses changing strategies librarians have adopted in dealing with vendors and how the vendors have coped with these strategies. Malcom Getz, Associate Provost for Information Services and Technology at Vanderbilt University, describes electronic tools which have become available to support collection development and their impact upon information acquisitions. Charles Hamaker, Assistant Director for Collection Development at Louisiana State University, continues his investigation of book and serial cost trends. His paper presents an indexing approach that complements studies presented at previous conferences. Robert Houbeck, Head of the Serials and Acquisitions Division at the University of Michigan Libraries, describes allocation process for library material acquisitions and offers some strategies for expanding the library's resource base. Carolyn Bucknall, Assistant Director for Collection Development at the University Texas completes the series of papers with an examination of libraries assumptions about "balancing" monograph and serials acquisitions and the strategies that are employed for maintaining the balance.

The papers invoked interesting discussions sessions during the conference. Unfortunately, this volume is not able to record the interchange of these ideas. However, we are pleased to be able to provide this collection of articles in the hope that it will give some insight into the issues that face libraries.

I would like to thank Wilbur Stolt who provided editorial assistance in the preparation of this volume, Don Hudson who served as conference coordinator and Pat Webb who provided secretarial support for this volume. Their contributions are greatly appreciated.

Sul H. Lee

Budgeting for Monographs, Serials, and Electronic Databases — How Should the Tart Be Cut?

Roger K. Hanson

Before launching into details perhaps the title should be briefly explained. The first sentence of the title identifies a very difficult process. The second sentence is perhaps a bit of cynicism resulting from dealing with inadequate funding for library acquisitions for several years. A tart is defined as "a small pie" and the acquisitions pie seems to become constantly smaller due to rampant inflation, profiteering, and demands for resources in new formats (and their associated ongoing costs).

In 1981, a paper titled, "Serials Deselection: A Dreadful Dilemma" was presented at this conference. In a sense this paper could be a sequel titled "Serials Deselection: A Dreadful Dilemma Revisited" since such an event again appears imminent at the University of Utah. Introduction of electronic databases as acquisitions expenditures is going to compound, and expedite, the problem of doing so even more.

Since there are not agreed upon formulas for how much of the budget should be spent for monographs, serials, or electronic databases, assumptions or guidelines should be established and explained to your community. Members of the community will vary according to type of library. The academic community can consist of students, faculty, administration, legislatures, and anyone else who feels they have a stake.

The Marriott Library has for many years used a figure of 60% as

---

Roger K. Hanson is Director of Libraries at the University of Utah, Salt Lake City, UT.

© 1991 by The Haworth Press, Inc. All rights reserved.

an upper limit for serials and standing order expenditures as part of the acquisitions expenditures. Although electronic databases and services are not serials, they should be treated as such because similar assumptions must be made regarding funding commitments. Once an electronic service is installed the assumption is that it will continue, so ongoing costs are incurred — and don't forget maintenance costs, depreciation of equipment, equipment obsolescence as new technology is developed, the variety of equipment needed because of incompatibility of software, etc., etc.

Progress is being made on networking CD-ROM databases. The Marriott Library has developed a networking capability. This will be explained in greater detail later. It is not simply the technology that is at issue regarding networking. Each of the vendors probably has developed their own software and indexing system to run on dedicated equipment so they will usually raise questions regarding copyright, licensing or other issues to assure continuance of income. I will comment more on electronic databases later, but before doing so, it might be well to give additional background history of acquisitions budgeting in the Marriott Library and other research libraries that creates the problem we are addressing today.

As stated earlier, the Marriott Library has for about two decades operated under the premise that we should not spend more than sixty percent of the acquisitions budget for material requiring a continuing commitment of funds. This seems to be a reasonable, explainable number although not scientifically derived. Chart A indicates actual percentages over several years for serials only.

There are many inconsistencies on Chart A that should be explained. The first two years of the decade the budget for serials matched expenditures very well. For the last five years there does not seem to be a logical interpretation of the data. It would appear that either the library subscribed to several more journals, or inflation was more than 50% per year in 1987-88 and about 65% in 1988-89. Neither interpretation is correct. The library paid multi-year subscriptions using one-time funds. This chart is a good example of problems in using statistical data.

Another type of material requiring an ongoing commitment of funds we call continuations/standing orders. Expenditures for this category average about 14% of the total acquisitions budget annu-

CHART A. University of Utah Comparative Serial Expenditures and Budget

Fiscal Year	Expenditure			Budget		
	Total	Serials	%	Total	Serials	%
1980-81	$1,271,569	$ 581,017	45.7%	$1,323,600	$ 581,000	43.9%
1981-82	1,655,196	700,960	42.3	1,540,000	689,000	44.7
1982-83	1,788,327	705,669	42.6	1,725,000	760,000	44.1
1983-84	2,055,006	758,396	36.9	1,725,000	760,000	44.1
1984-85	1,876,338	744,805	39.7	1,764,000	505,400	28.7
1985-86	2,208,167	978,547	44.3	1,800,000	869,800	48.3
1986-87	2,206,376	887,780	40.2	1,800,000	960,000	53.3
1987-88	3,075,359	1,239,560	40.3	2,570,000	960,000	37.3
1988-89	3,388,340	2,059,288	60.8	2,570,000	1,178,000	45.8
1989-90	Not available			2,540,000	1,260,000	49.6

ally. Adding 14% for continuations/standing orders to the 49.6% for serials indicates that 66.8% of the acquisitions budget is already committed, therefore efforts are being made to reduce the total to below sixty percent.

There are very explainable, although complicated reasons, why action has not occurred earlier. Part of the problem was optimism. The library was receiving a considerable amount of "one-time" money from legislative appropriations and other efforts. Library management kept anticipating that rampant inflation would decrease and that base funding increases were forthcoming, you know, the traditional pot of gold at the end of the rainbow.

Chart B is a summary of the Marriott Library's budget for the decade of the 80s.

The decade began very well with 16.3% and 12% increases for acquisitions the first two years. These years were followed by four years of, for all practical purposes, no increases. In 1987-88, following a major reallocation of funding on campus, the acquisitions budget increased 42.7 percent. This has been followed again by a year of zero increase and this year a 1.2 percent reduction. This kind of instability is what creates instability among acquisitions librarians and library administrators.

Probably serials cuts should have been made during the period from 1983 to 1987, but there were reasons for not having to do so. In 1983, student government leadership came to the rescue of the library and really forced the large increase in 1987. This experience has value you may all benefit by, so it is worth further elaboration.

The Library Policy Advisory Board (traditional library committee that is variously cursed or praised) at the University of Utah has six student representatives. Because of the library's experience of cancelling more than 1,000 subscriptions in 1980 and the possibility of having to do so again appearing on the horizon, this committee was kept well informed regarding the library's budget. One of the student members in 1982 became student body president in 1983. The earlier orientation paid dividends.

Soon after taking office the new student body president expressed concern about tuition increases and students having no choice or influence in the matter. He said, "I know we will be getting another one this year and if we can't stop it maybe we can influence how the funds will be used." After some discussion he and his colleagues drew up a proposal that they would accept a 2% surcharge on tuition if the legislature would match it 2-for-1 and the money be used for library acquisitions. They later carried this idea to the Utah Students Association, which is the coordinating group for student governments of all institutions. The proposal was supported, a legislative bill was prepared, dollar figures plugged in, and a legislator to sponsor the bill was found. The bill passed and the end result was $3,000,000 of one-time money for all institutions for library acquisitions. The Marriott Library share was $1,100,000.

The effort was not only greatly appreciated but very timely. Chart B indicated the years of no increases from 1983 to 1987. The $1,100,000 of one-time money helped carry library acquisitions through this period without journal cancellations and allowed time for the library to educate administrators and the public about problems that would occur when the one-time money was all spent. Chart C indicates the condition that was developing. The gap between budget and expenditures was large and expanding.

Usually one-time monies result from accumulations of unspent dollars during the fiscal year and often must be spent quickly. The result is not always that the best choices of material purchased have been made. The Marriott Library proposed to extend the time period for spending over three years with funds to be used for maintaining journal subscriptions and purchasing monographs. At the end of the time period the library was prepared for an extensive journal cancellation project.

In 1986, after hearing that higher education institutions would have to reduce budgets by six percent, our University President proposed to our Governor that the University of Utah would reduce its budget by ten percent provided the money stay with the university and be reallocated. The proposal was accepted and each department, including the Marriott Library, had to present its plan for budget reductions. A painful process.

Having been through similar experiences before, the process was well understood, but an expression learned early in my library administrative career is "don't let them cut dollars, make them cut programs." The meaning of this is that instead of stating dollars to be cut, put explanations in terms of services and programs to be

CHART B. University of Utah Ten Year Budget Summary Comparison

Fiscal Year	Salaries	Hourly	Total Personal Service	Acquisition & Binding	Supplies & Equipment	Totals
1980-81	$1,879,809	$463,027	$2,342,836(58%)	$1,323,600(32%)	$371,130(9.3%)	$4,037,566
Change	10.1%	-9.3%	6.2%	16.3%	9.2%	
1981-82	2,070,419	420,000	2,490,419(56.1%)	1,540,000(34.7%)	409,981(9.2%)	4,440,400
Change	6.1%	15.7%	7%	12%	8.6%	
1982-83	2,197,077	486,138	2,683,215(55%)	1,725,000(35%)	462,508(8.6%)	4,870,723
Change	0%	0	0	0		
1983-84	2,197,077	486,138	2,683,215(55%)	1,725,000(35%)	462,508(8.6%)	4,870,723
Change	7.4%	13.1%	8.5%	2.2%	10.2%	
1984-85	2,361,358	550,188	2,911,546(56%)	1,764,000(34%)	526,000(10.2%)	5,201,546
Change	11.8%	-2%	9.2%	2%	10%	
1985-86	2,640,890	539,500	3,180,390(57.5%)	1,800,000(33%)	541,410(10%)	5,521,800
Change	1.8%	7.5%	2.8%	0	.1%	
1986-87	2,690,370	580,220	3,270,590(58.2%)	1,800,000(32.1%)	544,910(9.7%)	5,615,500
Change	2.0%	-15%	-1%	42.7%	-5.6%	14.4%
1987-88	2,744,425	492,365	3,236,790(51.5%)	2,570,000(40.5%)	541,410(8.4%)	6,348,300
Change	1.1%	0	1%	0	10.9%	0
1988-89	2,774,863	492,365	3,267,228(51.5%)	2,570,000(40.5%)	511,072(8%)	6,348,300
Change	10.2%	4.9%	9.4%	-1.2%		5.2%
1989-90	3,0057,934	516,466	3,574,400(53.5%)	2,540,000(38.0%)	566,680(8.5%)	6,681,080
Average Annual Increase	7.0%	1.3%	5.8%	10.2%	5.8%	7.3%
1987-88 ARL University Average			52.2%	34.8%	13.0%	
1989-90 Univeristy Average			53.5%	38.0%	8.5%	

CHART C
Shortfall in Funding for Library Materials

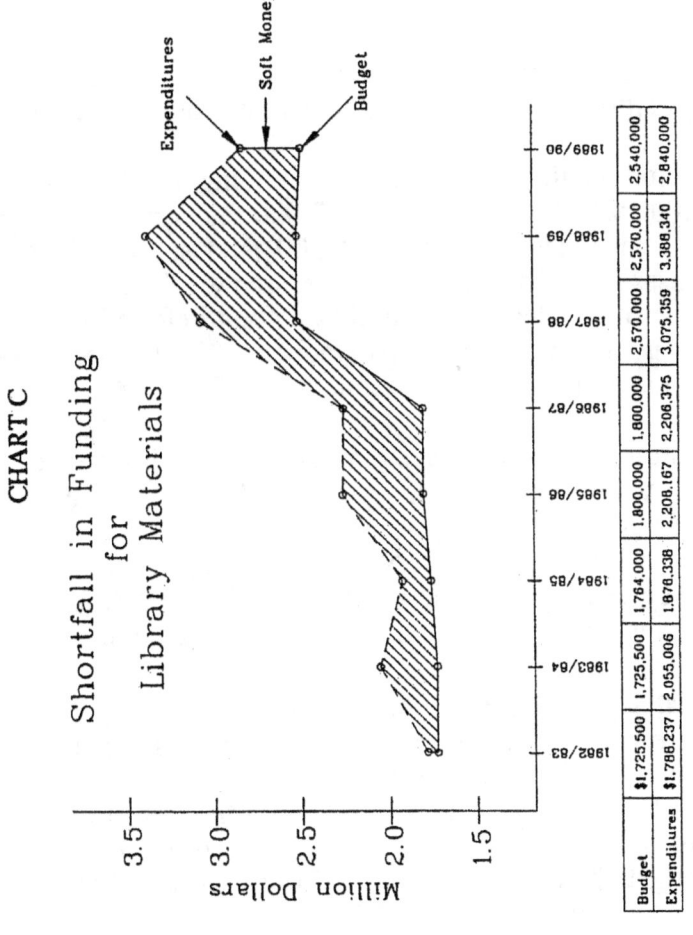

	1962/63	1963/64	1964/85	1985/86	1986/87	1987/88	1988/89	1989/90
Budget	$1,725,500	1,725,500	1,764,000	1,800,000	1,800,000	2,570,000	2,570,000	2,540,000
Expenditures	$1,788,237	2,055,006	1,876,338	2,208,167	2,206,375	3,075,359	3,388,340	2,840,000

Estimated Expenditure

eliminated or reduced. If library acquisitions are to be reduced indicate areas of reductions and the effect on programs. Prepare all the supporting evidence you can to defend your actions. Remember another adage "those who make decisions are hated, because they can be blamed."

The Marriott Library did prepare proposals for reductions. Included were:

1. Reduction in library hours because of elimination of 7.25% FTE positions. Total hours for the year would be reduced by 600 hours.
2. Reduction in library acquisitions funding in the amount of $360,000 which would result in 7,000 fewer monograph purchases, cancellation of up to 1,500 paid subscriptions, and purchases for individual faculty research would be eliminated. Because of the decreased purchasing and deferred binding of materials, the library could also reduce 4.25 FTE clerical positions thus producing a total reduction of $423,000 in this program.
3. Reduction in library services infrastructure. This category included cancelling some electronic databases because we still had the paper indexes; less use of the OCLC database for verification; slower mail delivery which meant current periodicals would be delayed in being available to library patrons; reduction in support staff to provide access to collections.

Substantial supporting evidence was provided to support the notion that there was no cushion in existing operations to make dollar reductions and sustain the workload. It was pointed out that through efficient use of staff, elimination of positions through attrition, and closing branch libraries the library had increased the percentage of the total budget spent for acquisitions from 27.8% to 35.3%. The Marriott Library presently spends 38.0% of the total budget for acquisitions compared to an Association of Research Libraries (ARL) member average of 34%. The ARL average percentage for personal services is 52.2% while the Marriott Library spends 53.3%. Under the "Other" category we spend 8.5% while the ARL average is 13%. Statistical data supported the library's proposals.

The end result was some reduction in personnel accompanied by reduction in library hours, but an increase of $770,000 for library acquisitions. Many people had the impression that the library had been "healed" after receiving this large sum of money. Not true. The average price increase for U.S. serials from 1978 to 1988 was 18.3% and hardcover books increased an average of 10.5% during the same time period. Referring back to Chart B, you can see that the average annual budgetary increase for the decade was 10.2 percent. This increase was still below annual inflationary costs so the library is entering the decade of the 90s with decreased buying power in relation to the beginning of the decade of the 80s. The tart gets smaller and maybe less palatable.

Perhaps more should be said about student government support of the library. Student government was given a lot of recognition for their efforts in 1983-84 and it was a very fulfilling experience for them and the support has continued. Some examples:

— In 1986, the Associated Students of the University of Utah (ASUU) provided $40,000 to purchase audiovisual equipment.
— In 1986, the university imposed a surcharge on tuition to fund purchasing microcomputers for student use. This they resisted because of the limited number of people who would use the equipment, yet everyone had to pay. Student leaders were reminded that almost all students use the library, so why not use these funds to install an integrated library system. They successfully lobbied for the project.
— An ASUU committee prepared a proposal later approved by the ASUU Assembly to fund purchasing CD-ROM equipment if the Marriott Library would raise matching funds. Using this as bargaining power, the library's match was funded by a local foundation.
— Several other smaller efforts:
    Buy-a-Book program;
    Parents Buy-a-Book program;
    Collecting aluminum cans;
    Recycling old 501 Levis;
    Dances, 5K runs!

These efforts are pointed out to emphasize who your best allies can be. There are fond memories of exciting working relationships with student leaders. Having been in library administration during the 1960s when students' goals seemed to be to destroy the library, this writer can honestly say it is more enjoyable to work with students who want to build the library rather than those who wish to destroy it.

The information presented may seem unrelated to the topic, Budgeting for Monographs, Serials, and Electronic Databases, but is presented as an example of how one institution survived the dilemmas of the 80s. Little has been said thus far about electronic databases other than installation of the integrated library system and the students' efforts to purchase CD-ROM databases. In a sense it was the student leaders who pushed the library into the CD quagmire. Since this is a new challenge for all libraries, perhaps time should be spent discussing some of the issues — and they are many and varied.

At this point, it is unclear how expenditures for CD-ROM services are being recorded by libraries. Are they being purchased with acquisitions funds? Are they charged against supplies and equipment? Or, are the charges recorded under that nebulous "Other" category? Regardless of which account they are charged against, it is likely that they will regularly increase as a percentage of the total budget.

In reviewing summaries of ARL statistics and assuming that automation charges are recorded under "Other," Chart D indicates percentage changes under three main headings.

It is noteworthy that the percentage spent for "Books and Binding" has remained stable. The percentage for "Salaries and Wages" has dropped, while the percentage for "Other" has increased significantly. One assumption may be that automation has made libraries less labor-intensive requiring fewer personnel. Of course, another interpretation may be that automation is costing so much libraries can't afford to hire more staff or increase salaries adequately.

The "less labor intensive" assumption may be inaccurate, however, because it appears that libraries will have to increase library orientation efforts to teach users how to access the multitude of

CHART D. Composite Average Expenditures by Category for Association of Research Libraries Members

	Books & Binding	Salaries & Wages	Other
78/79	33.3	57.2	9.3
79/89	33.4	56.8	9.6
80/81	33.4	56.5	9.9
81/82	33.1	56.2	10.6
82/83	33.8	55.1	11.0
83/84	33.7	54.3	11.9
84/85	33.4	53.6	12.8
85/86	32.1	52.8	13.1
86/87	32.5	52.1	13.7
87/88	33.0	52.2	13.0

electronic services. Funds from personnel savings in technical services departments are now needed in public service departments.

Libraries now have many years of experience using remote on-line databases for literature searching. The costs associated with such services have been quite high because of telecommunication charges, so most libraries have welcomed the introduction of local searching via CD-ROM databases. This "new kid on the block" is creating new and different problems. They will not be covered in detail in this paper, but some remarks are in order. The impact of CD-ROMs (or other electronic tools) on reference departments, teaching departments, students, and budgets is great.

Compact disc-read-only memory is likely the most popular technological advancement introduced in the past five years. Information is stored on a disc through pits and grooves that are read using laser technology. During the early years of this technology, the cost of mastering a disc was quite high, but now costs are only a fraction of earlier charges thus causing use of the technology to expand rapidly. In 1986, only about fifty databases were available. In 1989, this had grown to five-hundred databases.

One CD-ROM will hold the equivalent of about 200,000 typed, single-spaced pages, or the equivalent of about 1,500 floppy discs. Because of this, complete reference works, encyclopedias, and on-line databases can be stored on one disc. Since there are so many access points by which information can be retrieved, CD-ROM has a distinct advantage over printed sources. Printed sources are accessed only through their tables of contents and indexes. Perhaps the greatest drawback to CD-ROM has been that only one user at a time could gain access. This problem has now been resolved as local area networks are being used to connect CD-ROM workstations. Several products are available in a variety of prices. Each has advantages and disadvantages and it is logical to assume that those having the best features are likely the most expensive.

The Marriott Library has developed its own CD-ROM network using Novelle and CBIS software. Because of the large patron base the library wanted to achieve the maximum number of terminals on the network. The staff felt that turnkey or ready to run networks supplied by outside vendors are very expensive; therefore, the library chose to take more time to build an inexpensive network and use funds which would have been spent for a turnkey system to purchase more terminals.

The network consists of 21 CD-ROM drives on a network of 7 terminals. There are also three stand alone units. The stand alone units are required for those vendors not allowing networking. Terminals to access the system will be located in three departments on three different floors of the library. The CD-ROM disc drives will be located in the computer room. The system will be controlled by two microcomputers. One microcomputer will function as the network server and the other as a file server. Initially, the network will serve the designated microcomputers. The next step will be to extend the availability to microcomputers (150 units) in the library's microcomputer center and eventually make access available through the campus network. A major benefit of extending the capability to the microcomputer center is the availability of two microcomputer classrooms that can be used for training database users.

Without going into detail, suffice it to say that the need for orientation to access information services is greater than any time in the history of libraries. Many libraries may even establish a separate CD-ROM, or electronic database, reference desk—at least through a transition stage for a generation of users.

One of the problems already facing the Marriott Library—and it will increase in complexity—is what happens after a patron has completed a search. They may not have completed the search as well as should have been done, but the person wants a printout of the results. (Remember when we had to write all of these out by hand?) The cost of paper, ink, and other supplies will become a major expense for every library unless patrons are trained to become more sophisticated users. The Marriott Library is considering many options. Maybe printing will be allowed only after signing off from the system. There may be a limit on the number of pages a patron will be allowed to print. Patrons will probably be encouraged to download the information to a floppy disc or other alternatives.

Successful searches will vary according to the abilities of individuals. There is no doubt that machine readable services will place additional stress on reference departments. Patrons will need to acquire a different kind of basic skills in information literacy in order to effectively manipulate the databases with their variety of methods of accessing the information herein. A library has always been useless to illiterates; will it now be nearly so for those who can't machine read?

There are so many issues and concerns that each library must address regarding electronic databases and their role in information transfer. The question is not whether a library should provide access to electronic information, but rather how to integrate the new formats with our traditional printed formats into a cohesive information delivery system. If libraries don't do it they will soon lose their position as the major information provider on campus.

Over the past several years, libraries have seen the serials portion of the budget devouring more and more of the total. Now we are seeing the electronic media budget eating away at the serials portion of the budget which in turn impacts on the book budget. Institutions and their libraries are scrambling to increase funding and develop new funding strategies. Public institutions are becoming more aggressive in private fundraising. Usually this income is in the form of one-time gifts, but also in building endowments.

In 1972, the Marriott Library had three endowments totaling less than $30,000. In 1989, it has surpassed $1,000,000 in endowments with most of them developed during the last five years. Private fundraising has become a major activity. Student leaders have been very helpful in these efforts. It was stated earlier that students helped expand use of CD technologies, but they have also been instrumental in gaining funding. The ASUU Assembly contributed $25,000 from their superfund with the stipulation that it be matched from private sources. This was done and additional funding from other contributions was collected to establish supplemental funding totaling $120,000 to install the CD-ROM network and subscribe to databases for a three-year period without adversely impacting on monograph purchases or serials subscriptions. This will allow some time to gain experience, to establish permanent ongoing funding, and determine which (if any) existing print indexes may be deleted. In other words, the library is buying some time.

As stated earlier, the Marriott Library has received considerable one-time funding and almost non-existent base budget increases for acquisitions until the large increase in 1987. For 1990, the library may receive $3,200,000 in one-time legislative funding. About $2,700,000 of this amount is for library materials. With this substantial sum it is difficult to explain to people that the library may have to cancel subscriptions. Chart C pointed out the gap that develops when ongoing needs are funded using one-time money. A library also runs the risk of tossing good money after bad in supporting serial subscriptions for another year or more on soft money only to eventually cancel them for lack of funds. It may have been more beneficial to have spent the money on books. A book collection whose strength varies with the publication year as the budget goes up and down is likely not supporting university programs very well. However, the alternative of massive serials cancellations is not very acceptable either, so the following scenario is being developed.

Maintaining serial subscriptions has been a major problem for more than a decade. Untold hours of staff time are spent agonizing over which would be cancelled should the need arise. For the past two years, subject librarians have been working on dividing the serials titles into five categories, each containing twenty percent of the titles. Titles are ranked from "1" for the most important, to "5" for the least critical titles. The titles will then be divided according to two funding sources—those that would be continued on budgeted funds, and those that would either be cancelled or continued on soft money. A portion of the one-time appropriation would be set aside in a "soft serials fund." As funds from this account are depleted over a three-year period, serials would be cancelled according to the priorities established. The original plan was to fund the list for the three-year period and then do a cancellation. The alternative suggestion was to prepare lists to be cancelled each of the three years. There are important considerations for either alternative. Using the first alternative, cancellations would not take place for three years. Would this lead to administrative procrastination? Using the second alternative, attention would be brought to the issue at the end of the first year and, depending on community reaction, new funding provided that would then stop further cuts. This is not the type of "strategic planning" most of us prefer to engage in, but different strategies must be carefully evaluated.

In concluding these remarks, it is safe to say that budgeting for library acquisitions has become progressively more complicated from the 60's to the 70's and to the 80's. Budgeting and planning are complicated by the effects of inflation, the increased amount of material published, and the increasing subject fields and new formats available. How much should be budgeted for serials vs. monographs vs. electronic databases will vary from institution to institution. Each will continue to reach their own decision based on what seems most appropriate for them.

Earlier in this paper comment was made about several factors to consider regarding changes in information access, especially via electronic databases. These factors are not trivial and may have far-reaching implications for society. They cannot be answered today nor is that the purpose of this presentation, but it may be appropriate to pose the questions, either for discussion during this conference or a future conference. Many of them will likely be addressed by future speakers. Some considerations are:

—With leased databases rather than ownership what relevant product does the library have to show at the end of a few years?
—Should electronic databases be charged against acquisitions budgets or supply budgets?
—If libraries do not install the electronic formats will they lose their position as the major information providers on campus?
—Even if libraries do have the electronic databases, will individual departments insist they need them also?
—How does a library determine when to install a CD-ROM system versus searching remote databases?
—With so much material so readily available in machine-readable form will researchers confine themselves to the abundance at hand, foregoing information that would be available only by the tedious methods familiar to everyone?
—Who will be deciding what will be transferred to electronic storage and know that this is the best for scholars?
—If libraries charge for use of the databases are we creating an "information elite?"

The American Library Association Presidential Committee on Information Literacy printed their final report in January, 1989. Librarians, as information providers, should thoughtfully read this report and develop an agenda for action. We often hear the comment that libraries will be obsolete, that everything will be stored in a computer and we will be able to access it from any location. Perpetuating this belief may develop a damaging form of information illiteracy and our institutions may be producing graduates with a lot of "artificial intelligence."

The Challenge of Maintaining Research Collections in the 1990s

Jeffrey Gardner

Academic and research libraries have experienced enormous change during the past thirty years. The national commitment to higher education and research and development provided strong support to research libraries during the sixties when the country was responding to sputnik. Libraries' collection development efforts received broad support, the dollar was reasonably strong, research materials were—in retrospect—affordable, and research libraries' collections grew accordingly.

The seventies began to see the economic impact of waging the Vietnam War while trying to maintain a commitment to new social programs, and the nation's political leaders reduced their commitment to education and research. During that decade, research materials began to increase in cost as well as volume, the dollar began to fluctuate more erratically, and libraries began to experience serious difficulties in maintaining research collections.

Nationally, the eighties were years of economic retrenchment, reduced investment in our future through research and development, slippage in our ability to compete in the international marketplace and an apparent unwillingness to resist actively a future of diminished economic power. For research libraries, it was a decade of reduced purchasing power within the context of a continual struggle to maintain research collections across a wide range of disciplines.

There does not seem to be reason for wild optimism for the nineties. The country's leaders continue to back away from any mean-

---

Jeffrey Gardner is Director, Office of Management Services, Association of Research Libraries, Washington, DC.

© 1991 by The Haworth Press, Inc. All rights reserved.

ingful increases in our investment in the future; there are indications that universities and their libraries will face new economic challenges; and the nation's research and development effort will likely continue to be under-funded and focussed on politically motivated defense projects that do little to improve either our position in the world economy or our quality of life. For research libraries, the challenges of the eighties seem likely to intensify. Research publications will continue to proliferate, our dollars will continue to be relatively weak against the world's currencies, research and the resulting publications will become increasingly international, and the challenges and opportunities offered by new and emerging information technologies will increase.

A few illustrations of the current impact of these forces on library acquisitions place the problem in bold relief:

- since 1975, the percent of the universe of serials acquired by the average ARL library has slipped from 32.8% to 26.3%;
- since 1986, the number of monographs purchased by ARL libraries has decreased 19%, while cost per title has increased 38%;
- also since 1986, the number of serial titles purchased has remained stable while per title cost has increased 44%;

In essence, then, research libraries have been purchasing less, in spite of fairly healthy increases in materials budgets. And, the forces that have led to that situation will continue into the foreseeable future.

ISSUES FACING RESEARCH LIBRARIES

While there are indications that the rate of serials price increase may at least temporarily level off, there are also indications that prices of monographs are catching up with serials. In the past the cyclical nature of serial price increases has meant that periods of rapid increase have led to mini-rebellions by the library community which have led, in turn, to temporary reductions in the rate of increase. Currently, this seems to be the case, with the most recent ARL statistics indicating a current annual increase of 10% compared to the preceding year's increase of 12%. At the same time however, prices for monographs are increasing more rapidly and the pressures on libraries' acquisitions budgets are unrelenting. This situation has produced several consequences, including:

- Current collections are increasingly oriented toward the sciences and technology, with serials expenditures—largely in support of research in science and technology—averaging 56% of ARL library budgets;
- Library administrators have, in recent years, frequently faced budget crises growing out of serials over-expenditures and requiring either major shifts in library allocations, massive serial cancellation projects, supplementary allocations from the university, or a mix of all three responses;
- Publishers of scholarly monographs have reduced print runs, leading to higher prices needed to recover publication costs, and reduced availability of scholarly titles. As recently as ten years ago, the typical print run for a university press scholarly monograph was 1500—currently the number is more likely to be 350;
- Research libraries are acquiring less foreign language material at the same time that such material is becoming a larger and more important proportion of the world's publishing output. For example, American libraries' orders for material from German publishers decreased 20% over the past three years, and the Library of Congress estimates that it currently acquires less than 25% of non-U.S. publishing output.
- There is evidence that, as libraries reduce the number of titles acquired, they are beginning to develop homogenous, "core" collections, thereby reducing the nation's coverage of the universe of research materials.

At the same time that libraries' purchasing power in relation to published material has eroded, they are faced with technological developments and changes in the nature of scholarly communication about which not enough is yet known. New formats such as CD-ROM have been developed by publishers with little influence by libraries, and while many of these formats offer improvements in access, they frequently require expensive hardware that is not usually standardized among publishers. At the same time, libraries may be in considerable danger of becoming irrelevant to the serious scholar in the sciences who frequently keeps abreast of developments in his or her field through networks—either formal or informal; electronic or traditional.

The concept of networks is certainly not new—key scholars in disciplines have always maintained dialogues on continuing work. What is relatively new are the technologies and structures available for exchanging information. Scholars no longer need to rely on the mails or the phone, and the possibilities for electronic conferencing increase the number of people who can read and respond to research well before it ever reaches the formal publication stage. Particularly in the sciences there is a distinct possibility that the print publication of a monograph, journal article or technical report occurs well after many, if not most, of the key scholars in the field have learned of the research and responded to it (perhaps even influenced it). What has not yet occurred is any serious efforts at replacing the print publication as the medium for ensuring the proper attribution of the research, the distribution of appropriate rewards, such as promotion, tenure and research grants, and the retention of the research results for the historical record.

As electronic networks develop and become available to broad segments of the international research community, the nature of publishing and therefore the nature of research libraries may shift radically. It is, of course, useful to remember that the demise of the printed page has been being predicted for many years. Developments as diverse as the microfiche, digital storage of information, and interactive computers have all led, at one time or another, to predictions of the end of the book. As long ago as 1965, J.C.R. Licklider, in a still provocative book, *Libraries of the Future*, pointed out the tremendous disadvantages of books: they are bulky, carry more information than anyone wants or can assimilate at any given moment, are too expensive in the aggregate for private ownership, cannot be circulated efficiently, and deteriorate physically. Finally, they are fundamentally passive—that is, the book, the reader, or both must be physically moved for information transfer to occur. Needless to say, the library, as a collection of books, was not viewed by Dr. Licklider as especially effective.

And yet, through the years of rapid technological development since Licklider's book was published, the scholarly publishing and library communities have continued to behave much as before and the funders and users of libraries have not demanded anything very different. Questions that face libraries in 1990 include: how is the situation likely to change during the next decade or so, and what role are research libraries to play in designing and implementing those changes.

FORCES FOR CHANGE

Technologies for improving the process of information transfer have existed for at least twenty-five years, albeit in more primitive forms than today. What may be emerging is the economic, political and administrative will to apply these and other technologies to the process of information transfer. With the existence of Internet and the proposed development of the National Research and Educational Network (NREN), the potential for developing a national capability for publishing and distributing information in electronic form is becoming closer to reality.

At the same time, the role of users of scientific and technical information in promoting change and innovation in this area seems likely to become increasingly important as the scholar's work station becomes more common, as users carry out more of their own online bibliographic searches, and as the potential for radically improving the timeliness of delivery of research results via networks becomes apparent.

What has seemed to be a basic conservatism in both the research library and publishing communities is less apparent. Publishers have experimented with electronic publishing and while the results are spotty, at best, much has been learned about the process. It seems probable that for the foreseeable future, most scientific and technical scholarly material will continue to appear in print, while an increasing portion of it will be made available electronically in some way to a limited audience, in some instances prior to print publication. The future role of publishers and libraries in this process is not clear and depends to a large extent on those groups' willingness to be actively involved in developing the needed administrative, economic and political structures and processes.

In partial response to this need, ARL is embarking on a joint project with EDUCOM and CAUSE, the two primary organizations representing college and university computing centers. Called the ARL/CAUSE/EDUCOM Coalition on Information Resources for the NREN (National Research and Educational Network), the project will explore issues related to the development of an operational information network with broad capabilities. Initially, the intent is to develop the information infrastructure needed to share both bibliographic and textual material electronically. It is an attempt to move beyond an ad hoc approach to this development to one that will address issues such as: standards, intellectual property rights, licensing, service arrangements and cost recovery.

But in the long term, the most important issue may be to define and to assert the roles of scholars, colleges and universities, and academic and research libraries in the distribution of scholarly information. It is not clear what those roles will be—or even what they should be. Nor is it clear what the role of existing commercial and not-for-profit publishers would be in such a network. For example, it may be that publishers will continue to publish print publications while making digital copies available on a profit basis through the network. Or, research institutions may assert their ownership of the published results of sponsored research, making publishers more akin to delivery services, providing print copies of material already available electronically (not a prospect likely to appeal to many commercial publishers). The important consideration at this point is that the academic and scholarly communities retain essential control of the new delivery systems.

THE TRANSITION PERIOD

In considering the acquisitions issues facing research libraries during the next decade, it is difficult to ignore the present reality in favor of the desired future. In a sense, libraries have been in a period of transition since before Licklider's book of 1965. The potential for applying computer and communications technology to the information transfer process has been available since the nineteen fifties, and much has been done in the bibliographic area. The forces restraining similar developments in the full text area, are substantial.

Print material continues to be viewed as more significant than electronic material in the tenure review process. Academics and other scholars continue to play a critical role in the editing and production of journals, maintaining the editorial mechanisms within the traditional publishing industry. History and tradition contribute to individuals' comfort with the book and journal. And the international investment in traditional print publishing — by both commercial and nonprofit publishers is enormous. These, and no doubt other, factors will continue to drive the major part of the scholarly publishing endeavour for the foreseeable future.

Research libraries will continue to develop and maintain print collections, but will do so with the recognition that they must increase their strategic and financial investments in the future. As resources are shifted toward supporting involvement in and utilization of information technologies and networks, the research library community will need to continue current efforts at controlling the impact of traditional publications on their budgets.

This will require ongoing commitment to monitoring and influencing the price of traditional print material — both serials and monographs. There is at least anecdotal evidence that recent efforts in the serials arena have led to increased sensitivity of publishers to the threat of library reactions to inordinate price increases and similar efforts in the scholarly monographs arena need to be initiated. At the same time, libraries need to enlist their faculty and scholar users in efforts to define more critically truly important research and scholarship. It is important, however, not to become perceived as working to limit publication and dissemination of potentially important scholarly information.

ARL, through its new Office of Academic and Scholarly Publishing (OASP), will be working with professional and scholarly societies, as well as university administrators, to influence the academic rewards system to reduce the amount of redundant and peripheral publications. This is, admittedly, a difficult challenge, but worth undertaking as it has become increasingly clear that much of the academic and scholarly publishing output has become more important for authors seeking promotion and tenure than for readers seeking information.

For most research libraries, maintaining English language research collections has become a major challenge. If it is true that the development and maintenance of foreign language collections is a national need, then libraries and funding agencies may rediscover the value of cooperative acquisitions. Efforts are currently underway to secure support for an in-depth study of the status of foreign language collections in American research libraries with the expectation that such a study can identify strategic responses to what appears to be a major problem. The issue involves more than fulfilling the needs of current and future scholars; it is becoming a matter of reestablishing the nation's commitment to its own future economic development.

INFLUENCING THE FUTURE

If research libraries are to continue to be a major force in the scholarly, research community they will need to act collectively to influence their future. A major step is the development, as a community, of effective strategies for becoming active partners in developing new information networks which utilize existing technologies to organize and move information. Current efforts to participate in the design of appropriate uses of and standards for the emerging National Research and Educational Network are important first steps that can ensure a continued central role for research libraries.

The research library community also needs to intensify its efforts at persuading political and commercial leaders that we can no longer mortgage our future by short-changing our educational and research needs. While it might be alarmist to claim that we are a nation in decline, there are enough troublesome signs to indicate serious problems. Efforts to develop support for research libraries need to emphasize the contribution they have made in the past and will make in the future to the development of the country's capacity to invent, produce and compete within a global economy.

Much of this paper has been concerned with developments in the ways in which scientific and technical research is published and disseminated and much of the development occurring seems directed toward that audience. While the nature of scientific literature lends itself more obviously toward utilization of networks and electronic publishing, research libraries can play a key role in determining appropriate responses to the needs of the humanist and the social scientist. For the present and foreseeable future this requires libraries to maintain a proper balance between serials and monographs and to resist the temptation to emphasize the sciences that, we are often reminded, bring income to our universities. Research libraries will continue to be the guardian of Licklider's bulky, inefficient book—that anachronistic instrument that helps us to understand ourselves and the world we live in.

Libraries will continue to build collections of books and journals, even while it develops, experiments with, and implements new and exciting ways for scholars to share and influence each other's research and speculations. The challenge will be for libraries to retain their important historic role as keeper of the past while they design ways to become more active participants in the design of the future.

Monograph Collections in Scientific Libraries: Sacrificial Lambs in the Library Lea?

Daniel T. Richards

"The quality of the science and technology collections in America's university research libraries is deteriorating under the onslaught of stable or diminishing acquisitions budgets coupled with double-digit inflation. Over the past several years, almost all research libraries have been forced to reduce their book purchases and subscription lists to journals and other serial publications."[1] So begins an editorial in *Science* in August of 1981. "Much is made of the specter of journals consuming the entire materials budget of a library,"[2] says Sandra Moline nearly ten years later. Chuck Hamaker equated the purchase of each issue of a journal published by the major science publisher Elsevier with the non-purchase of a book.[3]

The introduction to the latest volume of the *ARL Statistics* (1987-88) states that "because of price increases, university libraries paid about one-third more in 1988 for the same number of serial subscriptions they had in 1986, and they bought 15% fewer monographs. It seems clear that ARL libraries are trying to protect their serials at the expense of monographs."[4] The same report notes that expenditures for monographs and other non-serials have increased only slightly in the past few years. Similar figures are cited in the recently issued Okerson report, *Of Making Many Books There Is No End*.[5] Lastly, Ellis Mount observed that "many sci-tech libraries have had no alternative but to cut back on monographs in order to

---

Daniel T. Richards is Collection Development Officer for the National Library of Medicine, Bethesda, MD.

© 1991 by The Haworth Press, Inc. All rights reserved.

keep major subscriptions to journals intact. It is not a happy situation."[6]

All of these observations illustrate that the continued escalation of serial prices has had a pronounced effect on the development of book collections in libraries. The problem has manifested itself in several ways, among them a downward trend in budget allocations for monographs, a decline in both the number of new monographs purchased by libraries and in the number of copies of new monographs available for purchase, and an increased awareness that resource sharing among libraries must assume an additional burden for what once were considered "core" materials.

It is my intention today to explore some of these concerns within the context of collection development in the science library. As I sought data on collection growth and changes in collection development specific to science libraries, however, I found few systematic data or statistics. Yocum[7] analyzed the situation recently and concluded that budget constraints are turning many academic collections from libraries in the traditional sense to working collections. Yocum's observation is ironic when one considers that it is from working collections—laboratory resources, if you will—that many science libraries arose. Dionne[8] addressed the impact of the declining purchasing power of materials budgets in science libraries, particularly at a time when exciting developments in technology are making additional demands on that same budget. But systematic budget data and growth patterns are not being compiled for science libraries particularly.

There is however is a wealth of statistical data about university and research collections generally, and information about science book publishing appears regularly in the *Bowker Annual*. Ballen Booksellers International has compiled and analyzed book trade data by subject and price for several years. Included in both of these sources are figures which illustrate publishing trends in science.

To provide a somewhat broader scope of data for this discussion, though, I am going to include as well some information on the health sciences and medical libraries. Data from these libraries—at least those in America's 115+ medical schools—have been collected systematically by the Association of Academic Health Science Library Directors since 1978.[9] These data are relevant for today's discussion because the literatures of science and medicine are more similar than dissimilar and their libraries have like services and collections. None of these data sources is comprehensive, but the combination can be used to establish a context for exploring the declining stature of the monograph collection in libraries primarily serving a scientific clientele.

It is my intention further to focus these remarks through the scientific literature—its structure and development, its growth rates and factors affecting those growth rates, etc. This is important because collection development in science libraries, as in most libraries, is predicated on some assumptions about the scientific literature, the most obvious being the fact that monographs are regarded as less important than journals. Further, in determining how well we are doing, i.e., collection assessment, we compare the existing collection with some segment of the universe of literature available on a particular topic.

As a side bar to the discussion about the scientific literature and because journal proliferation has such a pronounced effect on collection development in science libraries, I'd like to report the results of an analysis of the rationales for starting a group of biomedical journals. These rationales may help us to understand some of the base causes of this phenomenon. Woven into this section will be a brief look at the collection development process and library budgets, especially how the latter have changed in response to the growth of scientific literature and to serials price increases. Finally, I will make some observations and recommendations for resource sharing and cooperative collection development, how these approaches might assist us all in developing science library collections within the constraints of today's budgets.

A wag once observed that "scientists and engineers would be lost if the supply of journals suddenly disappeared through some disastrous set of circumstances."[10] One wonders how that group would fare if the same thing happened to monographs. Pearce[11] examined the development of the scientific library from a laboratory collection to a departmental resource and then to a substantial component of library systems. Convenience and proximity has always been a primary concern in the user's perception of the scientific library, logically, since the scientist spends such a large amount of time in the laboratory and turns to the literature at irregular intervals.

Alongside convenience has been ready access to a wide range of materials to support casual inquiry. It is this latter point which is of primary concern today. Another major concern but not one for today's discussion is the changing role of the science librarian as an information provider, particularly as one contemplates the development of electronic information delivery systems. Yeadon[12] in peering into the future sees an automated science library with librarians coming to "terms with the resulting loss of professional identity" once library operations move more completely from manual systems to electronic ones. No author, however, seriously suggests that the future will be "print-free" and that literature as we know it today will not occupy a central place in the information transfer process of the future.

THE SCIENTIFIC LITERATURE

The primary role of the literature of a scientific discipline is to record and transmit discoveries and ideas which advance the state of knowledge within that discipline. Another function of scientific literature is to help solve problems in the research process or the application of findings derived from research. The ability to do this is directly affected by the amount and quality of relevant information available. Scientific literature can be regarded metaphorically as a form of external memory from which we can extract and add at will. One may also view it as a structure made up of additions of small segments until a larger picture emerges. Ortega y Gasset postulates that "science advances by many small discoveries."[13] However one views it, that literature becomes a record of and for scholarship, hence, the "scholarly" record. Its completeness, or rather, access to it completely is a fundamental tenet of scholarship.

The scientific literature can be examined structurally in many different ways: by format, by subject, by date, by country of origin, by publisher, by language, or other device. To each of these one may apply importance indicators, particularly when considering format of publication. In examining the scientific literature by format, there are two principal levels of materials, each by its name reflecting in a real sense its relative importance within the literature. These two levels are:

> PRIMARY level material, which includes "source" documents, such as "true" journals, monographs, treatises, manuscripts, charts and maps, prints and portraits, and collateral "reference" items which contain original observations, e.g., annotated bibliographies, dictionaries
>
> SECONDARY level material, which includes all of the "synthetic" literature, or repackaging of the primary literature, made up of textbooks, reviews, popular treatments, annuals, handbooks, encyclopedias, indexes, etc.

A recent article by Tomajko and Drake[14] discusses the ways in which communication patterns among scientists are changing and suggests that these changes will alter traditional publication patterns and thus the familiar patterns of the literature.

Tenner[15] in the *Chronicle of Higher Education* reviewed the differences between humanists and scientists. He philosophized about the way humanists and scientists are divided not only by language but also by the form their work takes, i.e., humanists write books and scientists write papers. The reason for this is that "the pace of scientific discovery is too fast and results of research must be published too quickly to allow time for writing it all up at length." Others, he continues, lay the blame at the concept of specialization where the notion is that the number of potential readers (and thus book buyers) is too small to make writing scientific books a viable economic exercise. Kelland[16] explored through citation analysis the impact of monographs in the literature of vertebrate zoology and concluded that the average annual number of citations for books in this field was comparable to the citation rates for research articles, suggesting that the two forms of literature are of equal importance at least in this scientific field.

It is generally acknowledged however that the "true" journal literature represents the most important segment of the published literature of a scientific discipline, with monographs assuming an important but somewhat subordinate place in the literature. Libraries frequently make distinctions between textbooks and monographs in collecting. Textbooks are generally issued in a large edition which is superseded by later editions. They most often are general treatments of a discipline lacking the level of detail of a monograph. Most textbooks are based on the premise that education is a continuous process and are written with that premise in mind, i.e, textbooks are prepared to be definitive for teaching purposes but not for the discipline. Consequently, textbooks have a "shorter" life, affect by trends in education, by the popularity of teaching methods, and the changing importance of disciplines.

Monographs, by contrast, may be described as "ageless" and they most frequently contain a thorough presentation on a narrow subject. They have a permanent usefulness in a library, especially because subsequent authors may not undertake the same type of historical review. There is an attempt to be comprehensive within a restricted area which underlies the preparation of a monograph. One might observe that in general, the more specific and more specialized the topic, the longer the book is likely to be valuable in a library collection. Books in the specialties are likely to have a longer life than general titles issued in very large editions.

In *Little Science, Big Science*, Derek de Solla Price[17] plotted growth rates of scientific literature over time and concluded that the literature of most scientific disciplines doubles every fifteen years. He suggests that this growth rate has been relatively constant across disciplines. Price's theory has been challenged by others, most recently by Stephen Lock, editor of *British Medical Journal*, in the pages of *CBE Views*.[18] Lock notes that though there are something around 100,000 science journals being published, a substantially smaller number (he suggests 60% for biomedical journals) are "serious" and that the notion of an explosion in the literature is greatly exaggerated. He concludes that the annual rate of expansion has been a relatively constant 5-7%.

De Solla Price's theory does not appear to apply when one examines the rates of book production at the discipline level. A glance at some book production figures[19] [Chart A] shows that while the number of U.S. books in medicine published annually remains close to 3,000 from 1984-1989, the number for science and technology continue to rise. Analyzed at the discipline level, however, these same gross figures show widely varying growth rates. During this same

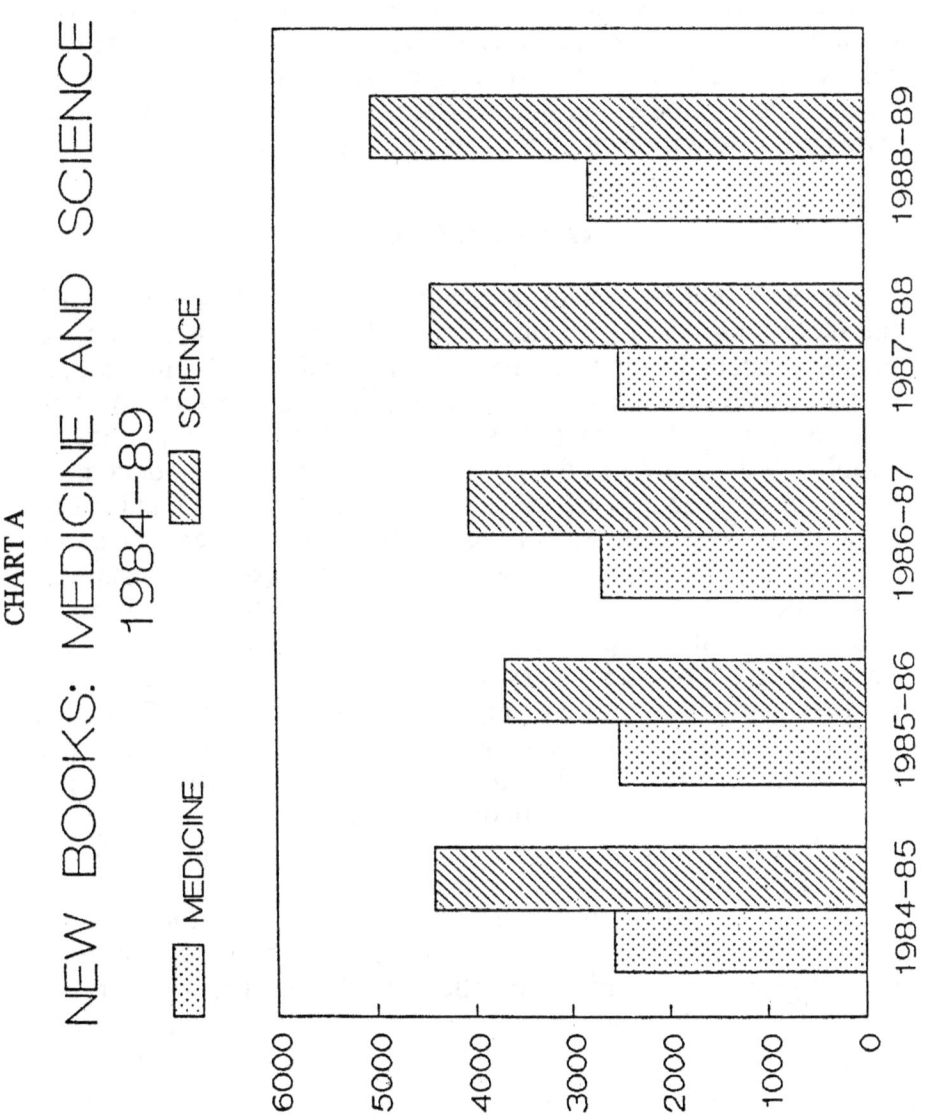

time period, there were nearly 1,200 books published in psychiatry for a growth rate of about 250 titles per year. The rate for chemistry was about the same but biochemistry was closer to 305 per year. Human anatomy by contrast grows as a relatively modest rate of about 40 titles per year, not too surprising since the subject matter is relatively constant. These figures do not take into account the world's book production but they serve to illustrate in a concrete way that different disciplines grow at different rates.

GROWTH RATES

Factors affecting growth rates of the scientific literature include the increasing cost of science, especially for instrumentation, the degree of specialization leading to fragmentation of disciplines, and the converse, an increase in interdisciplinary approaches to scientific disciplines. The changing and relaxed standards for publication coupled with an increased number of writers generating documents for the publishing mill affect the numbers of items being published, as do technological changes which have made document generation so easy, e.g., word processing software and desk-top publishing.

The document fragmentation syndrome which results from attempts to establish precedence in scientific investigation, also known as the "I-was-first" syndrome, can result in the publication of several articles where one might be more appropriate. The effect of tenure tracking and publication requirements—"publish or perish"—has been explored by others and its effect on publishing patterns is well known. Lastly, publishing mergers and changes during the recent past have diminished the number of trade publishers.

In 1800, there were approximately 90 scientific journals being published. By 1900, that figure had risen to more than 10,000. King, McDonald, and Roderer[20] demonstrated that the number of articles grows at a relatively parallel rate. The proliferation of journals led to the development of abstract and index services, which have grown at a rate of about 1 for each 300 new journals. The growth rate for journals in the U.S. has been very rapid but slightly lower than the world wide rate.

The growth rate for health sciences titles appears to have levelled off, and, in fact, is dropping. An examination of figures [Chart B]

CHART B

NEW MEDICAL JOURNALS
THE SEVENTIES & EIGHTIES

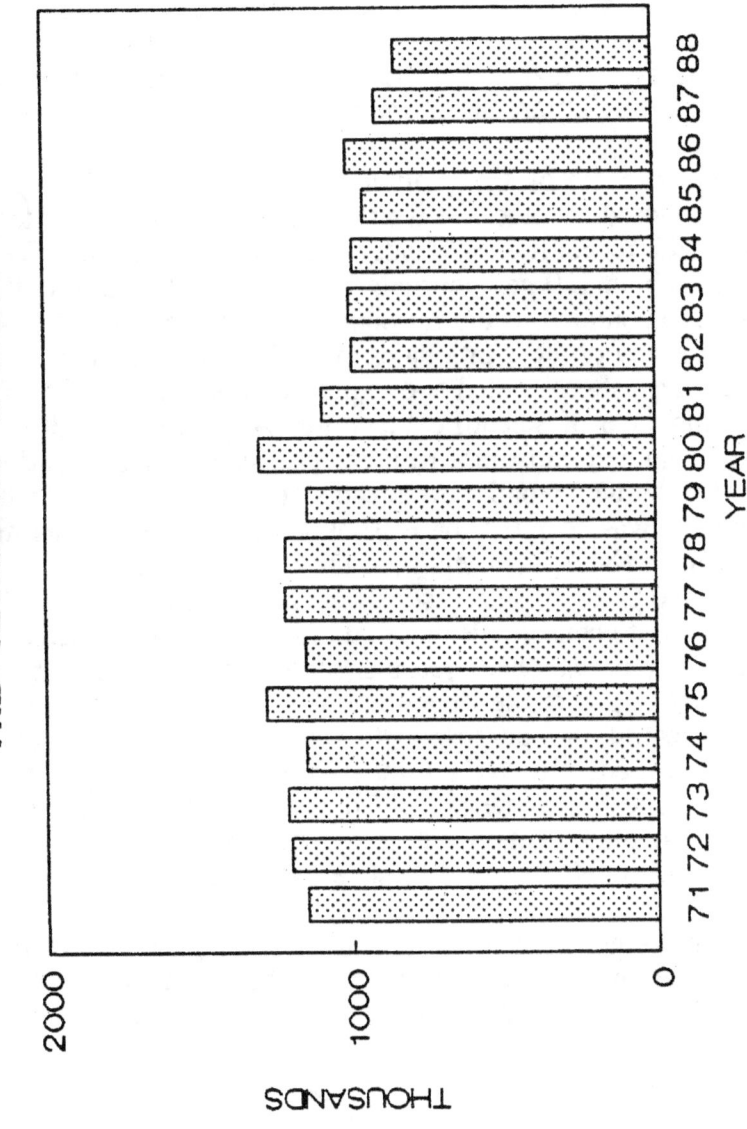

derived from SERLINE® suggests that though there continue to be large numbers of new titles produced each year, the number appears to have peaked about 1970 with nearly 1,400 titles making their debut in that year. The annual number had tapered off to about 150 by 1985, and continues to decline each year. Whatever the growth rate, the fact remains that there are large numbers of new titles competing for library subscription dollars and for space on library shelves.

Many aspects of the proliferation of scientific literature have been explored by others. I would like to share with you today the results of a recent review I undertook with a colleague.[21] We examined for about 150 new journals the rationales for starting the journals as expounded in the introductory issues by the editors themselves. Many of these rationales in conjunction with the changes in publishing patterns noted above provide additional insight into the changing face of scientific literature. Approximately 30% of the titles examined chose not to include a justification or rationale in their first issue beyond a masthead statement of scope. Each of the rationales was scanned for reasons and each reason was marked. Many journals included multiple reasons for existence.

The two predominant reasons were [1] to provide an interdisciplinary forum to consolidate material of interest which is scattered in a variety of publications, a reasons cited by 57% of the journals; and [2] "twigging," or the "maturation" of a new specialty, with several indicating that purpose of the journal was to bring about such maturation, cited by 51%. Almost as popular, appearing in 47% of the rationales, was the perceived need to enhance, speed up, or improve communication within a specialty or discipline. That so many editors felt the need to state the obvious we found remarkable.

Twenty-eight percent of the rationales suggested that they fulfilled the communication needs of members of a society or association. Smaller numbers noted the following reasons:

- To stimulate research in the discipline (14%)
- To synthesize or review the recent literature (11%)
- To educate professionals (10%)
- To improve patient care (10%)

- To publish abstracts or proceedings (6%)
- To meet the need for an "international," "American," or "European" journal in the discipline (5%)

Other reasons given by smaller numbers included these:

- To be a journal of advocacy
- To focus debate on critical questions in the field by inviting experts to present views
- To foster a new type of manuscript reviewing.

A similar analysis was done of two additional groups of titles which began publication in the 1950s and the 1920s. The predominant reason in the 1950-54 group was to fulfill the communication needs of members of a society or association, a reason cited by 80% of the sample group. Forty-seven percent noted "twigging" as a reason for starting, 33% hoped to enhance, speed up, or improve communication within a specialty, and 20% felt the journal would provide an interdisciplinary forum to consolidate material of interest which was scattered in a variety of publications. The same four reasons appeared in the same order among the rationales in the 1920-24 group, though with slightly different percentages.

When contrasted with the figures for the older group, significant differences emerge. Association publications account for the majority of the births of the older journals. This is not too surprising since many basic specialties and associations were being created during those time periods. What is surprising, though, is the large percentage of association publications still being born.

The other major difference between the old and new journal population is demonstrated by the categories which essentially do not appear as reasons in older journals. Before the information explosion, there was little need for interdisciplinary, twigging, or synthesizing journals. These categories have come about as a reaction to the growth of the primary literature.

The reasons for starting new health sciences journals fall into several categories, including both the splintering of disciplines and the opposite phenomenon—the interdisciplinary approach to a subject. Other reasons are to enhance communication or stimulate research within a discipline, to educate health professionals, or to provide a common forum to consolidate material of interest which is scattered in a variety of publications. Still other journals are brought into existence in connection with an organization or an association of individuals with common interests. It is almost axiomatic that an association will, sooner or later, produce some sort of newsletter or journal.

There are obvious differences between the reasons given for the birth of journals before the information explosion and for those which came after. Journals were and continue to be a necessary avenue for the useful exchange of scientific information. Before the information explosion in science in the second half of the twentieth century, there were few enough journals in existence. When a new journal was introduced, there was no thought of having to apologize for it. Large associations representing major medical specialties started new journals, and the specialists and libraries were delighted to play their part in their common goal of communication of scientific information.

As the information explosion progressed, however, existing journals could not handle the volume of submitted papers. Likewise, more and more subspecialists discovered that their specialty associations could not devote enough program time or journal space to their particular interest. The end result — new smaller associations were started; these associations started new journals; and specialist journals "twigged" off from their parent journals. As the literature became more difficult to handle, new types of journals appeared — interdisciplinary journals to bring different specialists together; and synthetic journals, to condense the literature to a more manageable level.

Scientific journal literature has almost become impossible. No library can subscribe to all of these journals, no matter how convincing the editorial. No scientist can read all of the literature, even if it all were indexed or worthy of publication. The perverse outcome is that new journals are created in an attempt to deal with the overload, throwing more fuel on the flames. As stated before, the principal aim of publication in the sciences should be to communicate new information in such a way that that communication expands or enhances the knowledge base. This goal seems at risk today because of the sheer volume of publication. We as librarians must be more certain than ever that our selections are judicious, appropriate, and add meaningfully to the collections for which we assume stewardship.

COLLECTION DEVELOPMENT

As new journals continue to appear and as they force libraries to examine and choose between them and the monograph, collection development and acquisitions are affected in profound ways, especially the ways in which the budget is spent. Collection development as a specialized function in science libraries is a relatively recent phenomenon, though the concept and the rubric have been generally employed in academic libraries for some time. Until the last decade, selection activities in science libraries have usually been subsumed under the title "acquisitions librarian" or have been regarded as the exclusive responsibility of the library director. The term "collection development" had its origin in academe, and was first used in science and other specialized libraries in the late 1970s.

Science librarians have, of course, been developing collections since the establishment of the first "science" library; but in the last decade or so, the processes, policies, and philosophies surrounding that activity have been scrutinized and articulated in such a way that a new specialty has arisen. The library's collection is the foundation upon which all other library services are dependent. Developing the collection is one of the most important — if not *the* most important — of pursuits in librarianship.

Documentation of selection principles in particular has led to the more systematic codification of the criteria governing the selection process. So too has the level of institutional accountability risen as the bottom line in the budget gets larger and larger. Budget planning and resource sharing are not necessarily new but are newly emphasized in collection development. Success in collection development today requires a more sophisticated understanding of the research process, of the professions dependent on the library, and, as previously observed, a solid knowledge of the creation and use of scientific literature and information.

A library's collections should be developed in a manner consistent with its overall goals. This process should be guided by a document which expands upon those goals, identifies the unique characteristics of collection development within the institutional setting, and articulates the policies and criteria which undergird collection development. So much for the ideal. Let us examine the ways in which the collection development process in science libraries has changed and what have been the effects of such factors as literature growth, declining budgets and increasing prices. The following catalog of changes is not comprehensive, and several have been raised by other speakers. The list, however, serves to illustrate the types of changes which have come about.

- The collection development process has become more reactive than proactive as librarians rely on the user to initiate requests for material. Collections therefore are being built in response to current needs rather than anticipated demand.
- Selection criteria are articulated in a more completed manner and are applied in a more consistent fashion. The inclusion of a journal in a major abstracting and indexing service, for example, has become a requirement for subscription rather than a desirable. Similarly, every other edition of a work may now be purchased instead of every edition. English language materials are almost exclusively purchased.
- Decision making for serials is being done more by committee than by individual selector and there is a heightened involvement of the user in the decision-making process. Maintaining the proposer balance with the latter is often a challenge.
- Approval plans for books in science libraries have been cut back dramatically and in some institutions eliminated altogether. Selectors are therefore seeing a smaller number of books from which to select and are thus not able to take full advantage of the primary benefit of an approval arrangement.
- A greater and greater proportion of the materials budget is being spent on periodicals. Earlier sources quoted by me suggest that ARL libraries are purchasing about 15% fewer books overall. It is my contention that in the sciences that figure is substantially greater. Expenditure rates for science libraries have not been tracked as a subset of ARL data. The AAHSLD figures [Chart C] noted before show the change in medical

school library expenditure patterns over the past ten years. Until about 1970 the typical medical school library budget was expended in about a 2/3-1/3 split with the larger portion going to serials. This figure was true as well for science libraries. The chart shows that the division in 1987/88 had reached 78.3%/21.7% with a downward trend clearly evident. This suggests a real dollar shift in the range of 23% and a greatly reduced rate of expenditure for books.

The net effect of these changes in collection development practice is a diminishing of the diversity in science library collections, ultimately affecting the ability of the library to serve the information needs of the local user—the scientist. Because this fundamental change in the nature of science library collections is occurring in many institutions simultaneously, there is a national consequence as well. The richness of the national collection in the sciences is eroding. The effect on scholarship and scientific research will be profound if solutions are not found.

I do not have a bag of magic tricks to address the problem but it does seem to me that cooperative collection development has some potential in this area. Building on the distinguished history of resource sharing will allow libraries to shape their collections in ways that minimize the effects of declining purchases and expanding growth rates.

COOPERATION IN COLLECTION DEVELOPMENT

Cooperative collection development occurs when two or more libraries coordinate their collection building activities in some agreed upon way. Such arrangements frequently grow out of a desire to use existing materials budgets more effectively. The goal may be to reduce unnecessary overlap or duplication between collections while maintaining or expanding the universe of materials available in the combined collections of the participants. Another motive might be to ensure that materials currently available to users in a given geographic area are not lost inadvertently through uncoordinated collection development decisions. Still other reasons for cooperating include:

- coordination of cancellations, storage, or preservation decisions
- enhanced understanding of the collection development processes in other types of libraries and coordination of planning for collection development
- the establishment among larger research collections of library of record status or primary collection responsibilities for specifically defined subject areas, formats, etc.
- distribution among smaller closely neighboring libraries of certain core or basic subject areas in order to reduce unwanted or insupportable redundancy, of particular interest to science libraries.

These potential reasons for entering into cooperative agreements can also be viewed as potential benefits to be gained from such arrangements. Mosher and Pankake[22] authored the recommended guidelines for designing and implementing cooperative collection development ventures among libraries. The rationales for cooperative collection development, as well as the potential problems, issues, models, policies, etc., are not significantly different for sciences libraries from those which affect other kinds of libraries. Consequently, this guide is an extremely useful tool for sciences librarians.

Cooperative collection development, or resource building, assumes a commitment to resource sharing as well. Resource sharing is commonly defined as the sharing of library collections through one or more of the following mechanisms:

- the provision of information on what cooperating institutions own
- the actual interlibrary lending and borrowing of materials
- direct service to the user populations of cooperating libraries.

Irrespective of the scope of the resource sharing program, cooperative collection development is meaningless without both a commitment among participating institutions to share their collections and an effective mechanism to do so.

Although the majority of activity in cooperative collection development has been among large research libraries, there have been

CHART C

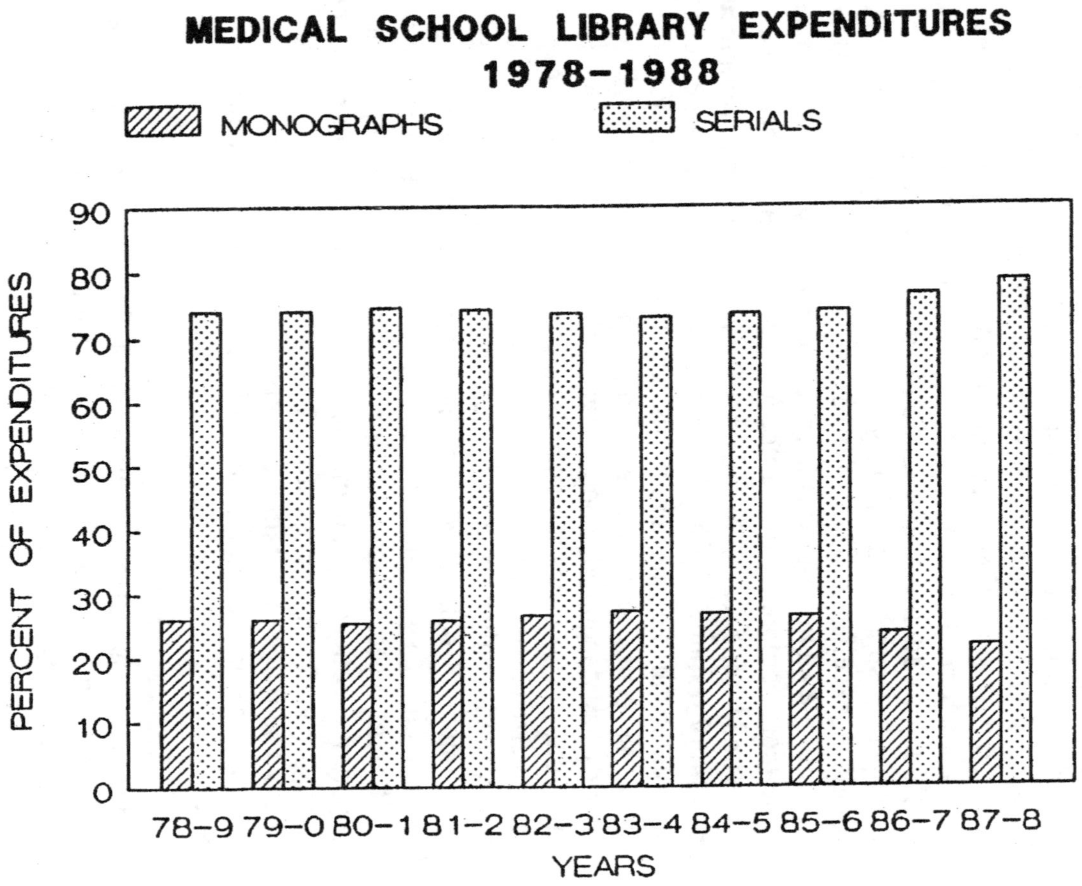
MEDICAL SCHOOL LIBRARY EXPENDITURES
1978-1988
MONOGRAPHS
SERIALS
PERCENT OF EXPENDITURES
90
80
70
60
50
40
30
20
10
0
78-9
79-0
80-1
81-2
82-3
83-4
84-5
85-6
86-7
87-8
YEARS

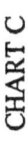

some cooperative programs in specialized libraries as well, notably among medical libraries. Cooperative programs with a large geographic base have arisen through the Regional Medical Library network instituted by the National Library of Medicine. Some ensure retention of important serial titles within a specific region; others expand the monographs available among health sciences libraries. These programs tend to include libraries of varying types and sizes. Even though the number of existing cooperative collection development arrangements among health sciences libraries is not particularly high, the administrative and bibliographic structures they have developed to support interlibrary loan and exchange of duplicates provide an excellent basis for further work in this area. These structures provide all librarians with a solid base upon which to build and refine more comprehensive collection development agreements.

The underlying reason for all cooperative collection development and library resource sharing is the knowledge that no single library can contain all the information its users need or want. While resources sharing can be viewed as providing access to what other libraries have acquired, cooperative collection development is an active attempt to influence what is acquired and therefore expand the universe of material available to be shared. If a library wishes to explore cooperative programs, there is no single model for such arrangements. Cooperative agreements can be developed among libraries within a single institution, among libraries of a single type, of different types, or along regional/geographic lines. Frequently, cooperative collective agreements arise among institutions which already have some other form of cooperative mechanism established. The range of possible collection development arrangements is enormous, but the requirements of the participants should include these:

- a clear concept of the mission of the institution the library serves and the way the library supports that mission
- an understanding of the present and future information needs of the library's user group
- a knowledge of the existing strengths and weaknesses of the library's collection

- an accurate picture of current collecting practices
- use data for the library's collection.

With the exception of the last of these requirements, all should be present in a well drafted collection development policy statement. Once these requirements have been satisfied, the library must decide if it has a reasonable basis for cooperative action in collection development. The probability of profitable cooperative collection development is more limited if the requirements of the participating institutions are largely overlapping and each institution acquires only core materials. A viable agreement must be a "win-win" proposition, and each participant must feel the agreement supports the individual library's goals and serves the needs of the user group. The parameters of an agreement must take into account a wide variety of concerns beyond the selection process, including processing, retention, use, fees, preservation. Procedures established should involve a minimum of additional work for participants and should provide a method for gathering statistics and costs for future evaluation. All of these factors should be reduced to a written agreement, much like a contract, which is signed by all parties.

The overall goal of any cooperative effort should be to minimize unnecessary duplication and to broaden the available resources. The success of the effort will turn on access to the material acquired under the agreement. The future for cooperation in resource building among sciences libraries appears to be bright. Many of the factors which prescribe cooperation will only increase and there seems to be no drop in the volume of materials in the information base. As science libraries find it more difficult to afford secondary and tertiary materials need by their users, the benefits of expanding cooperative agreements with other libraries will become even more apparent.

National and regional cooperative collection development programs have the potential to improve information service to scientists throughout the U.S., while aiding science libraries to make more effective use of their limited resources. Useful local arrangements need not wait for the establishment of national or regional programs, however. Individual science librarians can and should begin to explore local options for effective cooperation in collection building. The potential benefits to the science library and its users are real and deserve careful examination.

NOTES

1. Black G. Prospects for research libraries. *Science* 213(1981):715
2. Moline SR. The influence of subject, publisher type, and quantity published on journal prices. *Journal of Academic Librarianship* 15(1989):12
3. Hamaker C. The least reading for the smallest number at the highest price. *American Libraries* 19(1988):764
4. *ARL Statistics 1987-88; a compilation of statistics from the one hundred and nineteen members of the Association of Research Libraries*. Comp. by Nicola Daval and Celeste Feather. Washington: ARL, 1989. p. 7
5. Okerson A. *Of Making Many Books There Is No End; Report on Serial Prices for the Association of Research Libraries*. Washington: ARL, 1989. p. 13
6. Mount E. Collection management in sci-tech libraries: an introduction. *Science and Technology Libraries* 9(1989):22
7. Yocum PB. The precarious state of academic science library collections. *Science and Technology Libraries* 9(1989):37-46
8. Dionne RJ. Science libraries at a crossroads. *American Scientist* 76(1988):268-272
9. *Annual Statistics of Medical School Libraries in the United States and Canada*, 1st ed. - 1978- . Houston: Association of Academic Health Sciences Library Directors.
10. Stankus T. *Scientific Journals: Issues in library selection and management*. The Serials Librarian Monographic supplement #3 New York: The Haworth Press, 1987. p. xi.
11. Pearce KJ. Academic scientific and technical libraries: some 19th and 20th century tales. *Science & Technology Libraries* 8(1988):3-15
12. Yeadon J. The next ten years in the biology library. *ASLIB Proceedings* 38(1986):115-120
13. Ortega Y Gasset J. *Revolt of the masses*. New York: Norton, 1932. p. 23
14. Tomajko KG and MA Drake. The journal, scholarly communication, and the future. *The Serials Librarian* 10(1985/6):289-298
15. Tenner E. The "two cultures" and the decline of the scientific book. *Chronicle of Higher Education* 34(1987):A48
16. Kelland JL. The impact of monographs in vertebrate zoology on the scientific literature: a citation analysis. *Collection Management* 11(1989):77-95
17. Price DS. *Little science, big science*. New York: Columbia University Press, 1979.
18. Lock S. "Journalology": are the quotes needed? *CBE Views* Aug 1989 12(4):57-59
19. These numbers are derived from an unpublished report (September 9, 1989) to approval program clients from Ballen Booksellers International. The

report is entitled "Five Year Cumulative Title-Price Cost Analysis, July 1, 1984-June 30, 1989."

20. King DW, DD McDonald and NK Roderer. *Scientific Journals in the United States: Their Production, Use and Economics*. Stroudsburg, PA: Hutchinson Ross, 1981. pp. 7-28

21. Richards DT and ME Funk. "Apologia ad nauseam: an examination of rationales for new journals in the health sciences." In *Contributed Papers 1: 1989 Annual Meeting of the Medical Library Association; Session 2: Managing the Collection: Methods and Resources* [audiotape] Chicago: Medical Library Association, 1989.

22. Mosher PH and M Pankake. "A guide to coordinated and cooperative collection development," *Library Resources and Technical Services* 27(1983):417-431

Been Down So Long, It Looks Like Up to Me

Dana Alessi

Once upon a time, a long, long time ago (or at least it seems that way), libraries had money to spend for books and serials. They had more money than they knew what to do with. The federal government provided grants to build their collections. If they were state supported, their legislatures gave them money to buy books; if they were privately funded, their trustees dipped into deep pockets to provide the necessary funding for collections. Increasing enrollments meant more money. Campuses built new buildings for the librarians to house the burgeoning shelves of books and journals and microforms.

Students were happy; they had beautiful new buildings to study in and up-to-date resources to use. Faculty were happy; they could submit all the book and journal requests they wanted, not just for curriculum-related materials, but even for their very esoteric research interests. They could count on having materials in their library. Administrators were happy; they gained respectability among peer institutions and watched as students happily studied and faculty happily bought.

Librarians were exceedingly happy, if overworked. They could buy all the books and journals the faculty wanted; they could buy all the books their fellow librarians wanted too. They didn't have to worry about the "business" of acquisitions. They could be friends with the vendors who came to call and buy from those vendors whose personnel they liked the best or whose invoices most closely met their idea of perfection. They didn't have to worry about "the

---

Dana Alessi is Academic Marketing Director for Baker & Taylor Books, Bridgewater, NJ.

art of the deal.'' They liked getting an adequate discount, but they didn't have to worry as long as they could buy the materials they needed and balance expenditures at the end of the fiscal year.

Vendors were happiest of all. They smiled as orders flowed through their doors. Although occasionally one of their brethren vanished in the dark of night or very publicly in the middle of the day, in general they developed, grew, and expanded. They could sell the books they got from publishers at a fair, but not generous, discount to libraries. They could keep their gross margins healthy. They could sell to the markets they wanted. They frequently specialized by geography, by subject area, by type of press. Life was good for the vendors, for librarians, for students, for faculty, for administrators. Wouldn't it be nice if we could say that they all built, studied, taught, bought, sold, and lived happily ever after?

Unfortunately, the era of expansion of the 1960's and 1970's really now does seem like a fairy tale as we enter the 1990's. Librarians and vendors alike have emerged from the 1980's battered and scarred, victims of declining student enrollments, campus retrenchment, rampant book price inflation, stratospheric journal prices, and costly automation. In addition, scarce library funds must now purchase a wider variety of product options, i.e., video, software, CD-ROM, and an ever-growing number of books and journals.

Accordingly, librarians have had to change their strategies in dealing with vendors. These strategies have resulted in changes in the vendor-librarian relationship and have affected the way in which vendors do business. In the remainder of this paper, I want to discuss some of the strategies that I, as a vendor who has worked for two different companies and who has been both on the road and in-house, have seen libraries adopt in their dealings with vendors in the past several years. Since I have always worked for book vendors, my comments will address monograph strategies rather than serials strategies. Most of these strategies will be familiar to you; many you have assuredly used. I will then look at how vendors have responded to library strategies and how our own business strategies have changed in light of the new competitive environment.

One of the primary strategies of fiscally strapped libraries has been to seek a better financial arrangement from the vendors with whom the library deals. This more favorable financial arrangement usually assumes one of two forms: higher discounts or freight concessions.

When I first started selling books back in 1978, it was relatively rare to hear of any vendor giving a library more than a 10% discount, and frequently discount structures were significantly lower. For instance, one vendor estimated that the average academic library firm order discount was only 2-3 percent in 1983.[1]

Much of the past pressure to increase discounts has come from librarians who have analyzed invoices and who have not been satisfied with what seems to be minimal discount. They have threatened to remove their business from one vendor and take it to another if additional discount was not forthcoming. Believe me, there is nothing to put the fear into a sales rep's heart more than the threat of losing business to another vendor over discount. The wholesaler is caught in a squeeze—he is squeezed by librarians demanding more discounts and publishers who want to give less, faced with their own pressure to put more on the bottom line and to cover ever-rising expenses. However, as has been pointed out by countless vendors in numerous forums such as this,[2] he who lives by discount dies by discount.

To give you yet another indication of the problems the academic bookseller faces in terms of discounts, I've prepared some models to illustrate what can happen when even only one additional percentage of discount is given.

Table 1 assumes that you, the library, are ordering from a vendor four books from four different publishers, each priced at $40.00. You have a flat discount arrangement with this vendor of 10%. The vendor receives, for purposes of our model, a 49% discount on a trade title, a 33% discount on a sci-tech title, a short discount on a university press title. The association title you ordered requires both a prepayment and a publisher handling charge, which the vendor pays, of $5.00.

To acquire these titles, the vendor has paid for order entry staff, buying staff, receiving staff, stowing staff, picking staff, billing staff, shipping staff; he's paid for the sales representative who came to your library to convince you to buy titles from his firm and customer service staff to assist you if anything should go wrong with

Table 1

List Price	Discount to Library	Net Price To Library	Publisher Discount	Vendor Cost	Gross Margin $	Gross Margin %
40.00	10%	36.00	49%	20.40	15.60	43.3%
40.00	10%	36.00	33%	26.80	9.20	25.6%
40.00	10%	36.00	20%	32.00	4.00	11.1%
40.00	10%	36.00	0% + $5.00 Surcharge	45.00	(9.00)	(-25.0%)
TOTAL:						
160.00	10%	144.00		124.20	19.80	13.8%

Sample Gross Margin - 10% Discount

your order. In addition, he's got marketing staff and financial staff and data processing staff. His staff thinks it is underpaid. He's paid for supplies—purchase orders for publishers, envelopes, postage, invoices, boxes, packing materials, tape, labels. His suppliers keep raising their costs, and the U. S. Postal Service is once again threatening rate increases. He's paid for computer hardware and software. However, his hardware is aging and to keep up with modern technology he's going to have to invest in a new system. He's paid for telephone lines. He's paid for his physical plant-not only the building, lights, heat, and maintenance—but also for office supplies and well-worn desks, chairs, book trucks, and shelves. Plus he's got benefits to pay, conventions to attend, and a myriad of other expenses.

On your four orders at a 10% discount, he makes only $19.80, a gross margin of 13.8%. Quite honestly, that's not very profitable.

Now, what happens if you negotiate a flat 11% discount—only 1% more (Table 2). None of the vendor's expenses have changed, but now he makes $1.60 less, and your profitability to him as an account has declined to 12.8%.

Let's look now at Table 3. This time you are purchasing four books of the same type and with the same terms as Table 1, but the price is now $75.00 per title. Although your account is still impacted by the title which required prepayment and carried no discount, you are a much more profitable account to the vendor, not only in terms of percentage but also in terms of hard dollars. It will be much easier to negotiate with the vendor for a percentage point increase in your discount.

These examples are meant to illustrate two things: mix and volume. They are meant to explain why vendors continually are asking for a good mix, i.e., a good mixture of titles which will carry high discounts from publishers, although, as we all know, the academic library purchases few trade titles, with the bulk of purchasing being university presses and scientific monographs. Len Schrift has estimated that "the average discount enjoyed by the academic bookseller falls within the range of 29 to 32 percent."[3] These examples also should explain why high-priced sci-tech titles from mainstream publishers are eagerly sought by vendors.

Freight concessions are another method of lowering a library's

Table 2

List Price	Discount to Library	Net Price To Library	Publisher Discount	Vendor Cost	Gross Margin $	Gross Margin %
40.00	11%	35.60	49%	20.40	15.20	42.7%
40.00	11%	35.60	33%	26.80	8.80	24.7%
40.00	11%	35.60	20%	32.00	3.60	10.1%
40.00	11%	35.60	0% + $5.00 Surcharge	45.00	(9.40)	(26.4%)

TOTAL:

| 160.00 | 11% | 142.40 | | 124.20 | 18.20 | 12.8% |

54

Table 3

List Price	Discount to Library	Net Price To Library	Publisher Discount	Vendor Cost	Gross Margin $	Gross Margin %
75.00	10%	67.50	49%	38.25	29.25	43.3%
75.00	10%	67.50	33%	50.25	17.25	25.6%
75.00	10%	67.50	20%	60.00	7.50	11.1%
75.00	10%	67.50	0% + $5.00 Surcharge	80.00	(12.50)	(18.5%)

TOTAL:

| 300.00 | 10% | 270.00 | | 228.50 | 41.50 | 15.4% |

cost of doing business with a vendor. If you are paying 4% of an invoice for transportation (i.e., postage charges), getting the vendor to commit to free freight is equal to an additional 4% discount. However, vendors have seen the cost of freight rise significantly over the past years. Giving a freight concession is actually a more costly proposition for a vendor than giving concession in discount since his freight charges will keep going up and he gets nothing in return. As you have seen from our tables, however, a concession on discount can still result in greater profitability to the vendor if volume is high enough.

A second strategy libraries have used over the past few years is consolidation of business with a smaller number of vendors. Where formerly a library may have used four or five vendors for monograph purchases, it may now use only two or three, or it may have consolidated business with one vendor entirely except for those titles which it cannot get because they are foreign or must be ordered directly.

Although some acquisitions librarians may claim that their consolidation of business with fewer vendors is directly related to simplification of workflow within their acquisitions departments and with the turnaround time efficiency, overall fill rate and accuracy of the vendor, I believe we must also view consolidation as a conscious effort to wring price concessions from vendors and stretch budgets.

Two factors have made consolidation an effective strategy. First, many libraries now have automated systems which track vendor performance. This tracking not only involves fill and turnaround, but also discount. No intense manual effort is needed to determine what average discount a vendor is providing to a library; the computer can quickly figure the overall percentage the library is securing. Assuming that fill and turnaround are roughly equal, can a library afford to send its orders to a vendor giving a lower average discount in today's fiscal environment?

Second, consolidation of business, i.e., volume, allows a vendor to offer a library a higher discount. Consider Table 1 and Table 3 once more. This time consider the difference in business volume a library gives to a vendor. Assuming a similar mix, the $75,000 account is far more profitable to the vendor than the $40,000 account, even with a higher discount. If a vendor has a lot of $100,000 accounts, he may be able to raise his discounts still further because of overall volume, provided the mix is profitable.

There seems always to be a vendor willing to beat the price of another vendor (about which I'll talk a little more later), but librarians should realize that continually upping the ante as a condition of doing business is a dangerous game. Both John Secor and Len Schrift have predicted that no more than six to eight of the twelve major national academic booksellers would survive into the 1990's.[4] Fortunately, everyone is still surviving, but if any vendor is done in, a major contributing factor will be the razor-thin profit margins.

A third cost-cutting strategy on the part of libraries which has affected vendors has been attack on approval plans. The bloated approval plans of the 1970's have given way to the lean and mean approval plans of the 1990's. If you will, approval plans went on a diet in most academic libraries in the 1980's and shed more than a few books in the process. As vendors, we have seen libraries adopt varying strategies towards their approval plans:

- Cut back approval plans from books to slips entirely
- Change from books to slips to books within a single fiscal year
- Revise profiles to eliminate non-curricular related subjects
- Lower upper price limits where possible
- Request more frequent management information, especially information regarding estimated cost of plan
- Return more books
- Eliminate books of foreign origin from the profile
- Eliminate all peripheral modifiers, or non-subject parameters
- Change to publisher-based profiles from comprehensive publisher profiles

In every case, the net effect has been to limit the scope of the approval plan in order to spend the same amount of dollars or to increase at no more than the rate of inflation in order to free up money for firm order purchases. Since approval plans are a cost-effective method of new book supply for the vendor, approval plan cuts have impacted vendors. Faced with fixed costs of approval operations, they must now create new market opportunities for this entrenched and valuable service.

A fourth strategy to cut costs which has impacted vendors is what seems to be a trend towards buying more paperback books, especially if the differential in price is significant. And differential in price can be significant, indeed. For examples, I searched the "New Scholarly Books" column in a recent issue of *The Chronicle of Higher Education*[5] I found, for instance, a title published by the University of Wisconsin Press, *In Pursuit of a Scientific Culture: Science, Art, and Society in the Victorian Age*, by Peter Allan Dale, priced at $42.50 hardcover and $17.50 paperback. Another title, *Jean Baudrillard: From Marxism to Postmodernism and Beyond*, by Douglas Kellner, was published by Stanford University Press at a price of $35.00 hardcover and $11.95 paperback. There were several other instances of equally amazing price differentials. How many of you would have purchased the paperback editions? How many of you have policies in your libraries to deal with hard and paper price differentials? What determines whether you buy a paperback or hardback edition?

How does whether you buy a paperback or not affect a vendor? I return once more to our earlier tables. The lower the price, the less the vendor makes. Additionally, most vendors, especially if they are supplying approval plan titles, are purchasing hard cover editions, which can have inventory implications if you return the hard cover supplied on approval to purchase the paper edition—or order a paper edition which the vendor has to order from the publisher, even though he has the book you want—in hard cover—in stock.

The "one-stop shopping" concept is another strategy libraries are using in their battle against shrinking budgets. "One-stop shopping" is very similar to using fewer vendors, because that is, in essence, what the library is doing. However, whereas I defined consolidation as a reduction of vendors providing the *same* service, e.g., firm orders, "one-stop shopping" is a reduction of vendors providing different services. It is, if you will, a return to the "all eggs in one basket" syndrome. For instance, instead of having standing orders with one vendor, an approval plan with another, and firm orders with two or three more, so that the business is spread around, the library bestows its business on just one lucky vendor. Because the volume of business the library is giving the vendor is frequently sizable, the vendor can afford to sweeten the pot with extra discount.

There are risks with "one-stop shopping" for both librarian and vendor. Some librarians may still be mindful of 1974 and the demise of the Richard Abel Company. If "one-stop shopping" appeals to you as a librarian, be very certain that your vendor has strong financial resources. For the vendor, who must service many customers, there is the danger that excessive attention to the needs of a few customers because of the volume involved will impact the services given to his remaining customers. Because the volume of a few large customers can contribute so much to bottom line profitability, especially of a smaller firm, excessive care must be taken with that customer to keep the volume coming. While the "one-stop shopping" customer inevitably benefits from consolidation, especially if the volume is large, it can be a mine-field for the vendor.

"Value-added services" have become the latest buzzword when speaking of dealing with vendors and represent yet another strategy for saving money. Value-added services can represent a plethora of benefits:

- Reports
- Standing orders
- Reports
- Toll-free ordering, via fax or telephone
- Cataloging and processing
- Bar-code availability
- Lease plan services
- Management information
- Reinforced bindings
- Electronic ordering
- Machine readable records
- Approval and standing order microfiche
- Retrospective collection development services
- Publications

Many of the value-added services of book vendors are free or at least less expensive than if the library purchased the service from a different type of vendor. Although the library may pay for the service, because of economies of scale, the service may cost less than what the library would ultimately pay if it had to perform the service itself.

A seventh strategy libraries have used to husband scarce funds has been to take business away from vendors and purchase directly from publishers, especially if the publishers are offering a higher percentage of discount. While certain publishers, e.g., Bowker, have forced libraries to purchase direct, others have made discounts so attractive to libraries that purchasing from a vendor cannot be justified on price alone.

As Edna Laughrey documented so well in her study of acquisition costs,[6] however, direct purchasing is far more costly than purchasing from a vendor when factors such as staff costs, prepayment processes, systems storage capacity, etc. are factored in.[7] Publishers' costs too must be more expensive if servicing libraries directly. It costs a great deal of money to maintain small accounts; there are no ordering, billing, or shipping efficiencies. At least one publisher who has hitherto been most aggressive in promoting direct ordering to libraries has begun to question its past methodology; I suspect others will follow as publishers too seek every method possible to cut costs and remain profitable.

Most of the strategies I have discussed up to this point have been internal strategies, steps the library can undertake independently of external forces. Two growing strategies involving external forces deserve note, however.

The first is the growing use of formal bids and contracts for the academic institution. To give you some idea of the scope of growth, the dollar volume of bids Baker & Taylor Books has been required to bid on only for academic libraries tripled between 1985 and 1989. And that doesn't include the Texas contract!

Those of you from Texas state institutions have long lived with the bid process, both for the overall state book contract and individually, within your institutions, for approval plan and standing order bids. Minnesota has a similar contract structure for the state university system. Those of you from Oklahoma also live in a contract state, but one which offers some flexibility with an approved vendor list. Ohio has long had an approved vendor list and bids for approval plans for academic institutions, and Hawaii also requires bids. And now we have Virginia, which for the past year and a half has required each state supported academic institution to submit separate formal bids for firm orders, standing orders, approval plans, and periodicals.

What does this mean for the library? Possibly a higher discount, as bids are frequently awarded on price, although other considerations, such as service and automation requirements, may ultimately determine the award. Certainly it means a lot more work for the library as it prepares bid specifications, reviews vendor responses, changes vendors if a vendor with whom it does not do business is the successful bidder, and monitors performance.

What does bidding mean for the vendor? Probably a lower percentage gross margin, as price counts in any bid. Probably a higher volume due to the consolidation of orders. Certainly it means a lot more work as there are bid conferences to attend, detailed proposals to write, extensive documentation to provide, and careful quality control procedures to insure that individual bid specifications are met. Sometimes there are additional financial ramifications, especially if a significant performance bond is required. Sometimes, there are some good ideas as libraries incorporate "wish-lists" into bids which become core services and are extended to other segments of the market. And sometimes consternation at what seem to be impossible and fanciful demands, specifications that NO vendor can provide.

For private institutions or those which are not part of a state system requiring bids, the consortia approach to purchasing may offer an attractive strategy to cope with stretched funds. The most successful of the consortia approach to purchasing exists in North Carolina, described in detail by Jonathan A. Lindsey in his 1981 article, "Vendor Discounts to Libraries in a Consortium," in *Library Acquisitions: Practice and Theory*[8] and concisely described by Kent Hendrickson in a subsequent speech:

> Each year acquisitions librarians representing some 40 institutions of higher education meet with wholesaler representatives to discuss service and discounts. From the group of wholesalers who choose to attend the meeting, two are selected for the approved list. Each agrees to provide a specified discount

for all firm orders for a one year period. The wholesalers are evaluated on the basis of service provided and at the end of 12 months a new round of negotiations takes place. The attraction for vendors is a potentially large market for firm orders. For the individual library there are several benefits; (1) guaranteed discounts; (2) interaction with other libraries in the vendor review process (3) increased contact with vendors; and (4) since the contract is not binding, the library is free to deal with other wholesalers if service is not acceptable from either of the vendors on the list.[9]

Five Texas private academic libraries have recently banded together in a similar consortial arrangement, although their scope encompasses more than purchasing, including such traditional cooperative components as interlibrary loan. Other consortia of this type can be found in Oregon among private academic libraries and in Illinois, with a multi-type purchasing arrangement among libraries in the Chicago suburban area. It is very possibly a growing trend.

It is clear from the strategies libraries have adopted in this time of fiscal stringency that had vendors continued to operate as they did at the beginning of the decade of the 1980's, many would not still be in business. Just as libraries have had to buy smarter, vendors have had to sell smarter. Accordingly, vendors have also adopted several strategies to survive.

In his article, "A Period of Adjustment: Planning and Coping with Decreasing Funds in Libraries for Acquiring Monographs and Serials—a Vendor Perspective," Len Schrift characterizes vendors as falling into two groups as they face shrinking library dollars, a lower percentage of monographic purchases, and higher costs—the Reacting Group and the Responding Group.[10] Schrift characterizes the Reacting Group as usually small to medium size firm order vendors who use aggressive discounting as the only method they know to retain market share and sales volume.[11] Both Schrift and John Secor decry the practice of "buying the business" noting that the losers in any war of discounting will be not only the vendors whose service will ultimately deteriorate, but also librarians who may gain in the short term but will lose in the long term.[12] Regardless of these and other warnings both public and private, aggressive pricing has been a strategy many vendors have used to respond to the current competitive environment. This aggressive pricing most frequently takes the form of higher discounts, but, as noted earlier, can also include freight concessions. Both are short term strategies which will ill serve both libraries and vendors.

In addition to discounts and freight concessions, many vendors offer deposit account options, whereby the library deposits a certain sum with the vendor and receives interest or increased discount in return. This option, an excellent strategy for the library seeking to protect unexpended funds at the close of a fiscal year, offers a win-win situation. The library gets additional discount or interest approximating the rate of return in the money market; the vendor has a committed amount of business from a library and is able to invest the money the library puts up front and earn interest from that. It cannot be construed as "buying the business."

Another strategy related to pricing which vendors have adopted relates to service charges. If you remember our example of the title which had to be prepaid with a service charge from Table 1, the vendor lost money on supply of that title by giving a flat discount. We, as vendors, are frequently willing to make that concession since we know with a flat discount we will recoup the loss of money on one title through a higher margin on another title and since we are all committed to supplying the academic market with *any* title libraries need. However, on a sliding scale discount, unless we are willing to lose a little money on the assumption of a good mix, there is no choice but to charge a service charge to the library for acquiring this type of material.

A second strategy vendors have used to gain competitive edge has been development — and aggressive promotion of — value-added services. While libraries have looked to vendors to provide value-added services, vendors have responded by committing company resources to development of these services.

Three value-added services deserve particular note: the development of PC based acquisitions software, electronic order transmission, and the supply of MARC records, either with or without fiscal information with firm orders and approval shipments. Joseph W. Barker, in a survey for the Acquisitions Librarians/Vendors of Library Materials Discussion Group at the ALA Midwinter Conference, 1989, identified five different types of vendor-library electronic ordering:

1. FAX, E-Mail, and cataloging-utility-based ordering systems, whereby orders are transmitted from library to electronic mailbox, which the vendor accesses. This involves rekeying the library order into the vendor's computer.
2. Transmission of orders directly from a PC-based system into the vendor's own computer. There is no rekeying except for problem orders.
3. Interactive batch mode. Identical to 2 except the vendor returns confirmation of each order.
4. On-line interaction, whereby the library has access to the vendor's own database.
5. Interactive batch mode or on-line interaction with fund accounting.[13]

At the time of Mr. Barker's article, all vendors with basic PC ordering software provided it at no charge, and only a couple of vendors charged for the telecommunications fees.[14] Mr. Barker's final comment, "As we discuss electronic ordering . . . we should be sure we should all strive for *de*creased costs"[15] represents the dilemma the vendor has in supplying value-added services. On the one hand, if he doesn't supply value-added services such as electronic ordering, he stands to lose out to those vendors who do; on the other hand, the development of the services librarians indicate they want and need represents an enormous investment of company resources with little hope of true financial return.

The growing interest in receiving MARC records from book vendors to accompany firm order or approval shipments represents the latest salvo in the battle of value-added services. Due to their fiscal and technological resources, the larger vendors are much better positioned to provide the value-added services libraries seek.

Evaluation of inventory represents a third strategy of vendors as a response to the changing face of bookselling. This evaluation may take several directions.

First, a vendor may decide to establish agency plans with certain publishers. The vendor commits to acquire a certain number of copies per title in order to raise discount from the publisher. This discount may or may not be passed on to libraries.

A second method of inventory management is to seek to "turn" the inventory more frequently. This may involve both lower quantity buys as well as more frequent returns to publishers of unsold titles. What this means for the library is that delay in ordering a book may mean a longer wait since the title will not be in the vendor's stock.

A third method of inventory management may be to eliminate any inventory of short discount materials (i.e., materials with a publisher discount of less than 20%). What that means for you, as a librarian, is that you'll have to wait for supply of those titles too since your jobber may not have them in stock.

Vendors have altered their target market sales and marketing efforts as a result of chasing after fewer dollars. I see this reflected in two areas—the sales force and advertising.

When I first began my career as a traveling bookselling librarian, I can remember a vendor telling me what a cushy job I had—that traveling around visiting one's friends in libraries was a truly great way to make a living. Yes, the territory I traveled was large, but the customer base, at that time, was relatively small. I averaged eight or nine calls per week servicing existing accounts and calling on prospective customers. I was expected to be on the road no more than 50%, including conventions and sales meetings. No particular quotas were set for number of sales calls as long as my sales went up.

But two things happened—and not just in my company. If one is successful, one's customer base expands. The sales rep has to keep visiting current customers, but continue looking for prospective ones as well. Automatically sales call productivity has to increase and the ante is upped every time the sales rep becomes more successful. Unfortunately, territory size rarely goes down, so the rep finds himself or herself on a treadmill, trying to get to more and more customers and more and more prospects in the same amount of time.

The second relates to the competitive environment. Sales managers are simply requiring that reps be more productive in making sales calls due to both the business environment and the increasing cost of keeping a rep on the road. Fifty percent travel is a rarity now; I believe most sales reps in attendance here today will attest to spending anywhere from 65-75% of their time on the road. The luxury of the nine-call week is now, for most, only a memory, with a norm of twelve to fifteen calls now expected. Meeting these quotas is much easier, obviously, if one is based in a geographic territory which has limited distances between institutions; for the western based reps, it's a far different proposition.

And, in at least a few instances, vendors have moved to increase the overall number of sales representatives in order to get broader coverage of institutions and reduce territory.

Advertising is another strategy vendors have used in their sales and marketing efforts. To get a perspective on what has happened in terms of advertising, I looked at some journals, notably *Library Acquisitions, Practice and Theory*, *College and Research Libraries*, and *Library Resources and Technical Services* over the past several years. I had expected to find that vendors were advertising more than ever. What I discovered was somewhat inconsistent. Indeed, some vendors are advertising more frequently—not only large vendors, but also smaller vendors. However, other vendors who are still very much in business seem to have cut advertising from their budgets entirely, or at least cut back to only one or two ads per year. Those vendors who do advertise consistently seem more likely to take full page advertisements. There is greater use of four-color. Most of the ads seem unimaginative and stale, especially when compared to periodicals and systems vendors. Whether advertising is useful and effective is, I think, an interesting point we might wish to pursue during discussion.

Given that there are only around 4,000 academic institutions in the United States, and so only a limited amount of money to go around for the dozen vendors pursuing this market, two further strategies deserve note: market extensions and product extensions.

While most academic vendors will tell you that they remain committed to their core market (and for many that core market is the domestic medium-size university to the ARL institution), increasingly vendors are turning up in the strangest places. Vendors hitherto considered "academic" and concentrating on that market now arduously pursue other markets where there is logical spillover from the services they offer to their core academic clientele; thus, formerly traditional "academic" vendors may also have a healthy base of public, medical, legal, and corporate customers.

Vendors have also discovered the lucrative international market. The international market is particularly attractive at a time when budgets at U.S. libraries are stagnant. Foreign libraries are used to paying a marked-up price for their U.S. books if they purchase them from local suppliers. The American vendor need not discount at the rate he discounts for his U.S. customers, and he knows he'll be able to recoup most, if not all, of his freight charges. The foreign library knows it's getting a good deal because it will get books it wants at less than it would ordinarily have to pay; the U.S. vendor gets a better profit margin. For those vendors actively pursuing the international market, it is not out of line to state that the international market can account for fully one-third of the business. In fact, one major vendor has stated that 40% of its business is international.[16]

Likewise, as vendors have extended market, many have also extended product. For just a few examples in the 1980's, one can cite Baker & Taylor Books moving into the supply of audio and video; Blackwell's moving into domestic periodical services; Midwest Library Service expanding the scope of its standing order list; Yankee Book Peddler expanding from a university press approval plan to a full service plan in the late 1970's; and Academic Book Center/ Scholarly Book Center moving from a limited publisher approval plan to a comprehensive approval plan. I'm sure you can probably think of other examples. Product extension offers an opportunity to get additional sales volume from a core base of customers as well as to offer something additional to which non-customers might be attracted. If it is a logical extension of the vendor's business, return on minimal investment can be highly attractive.

If all of the above strategies fail, we are left with mergers, acquisitions, and bankruptcies. In the 1980's, we saw the disappearance of regionals like Academic Book Service and Siler's. We saw Scholarly Book Center dissolve in Illinois and take over the Taylor-Carlyle name in New York. We have just recently seen Blackwell's acquisition of Menzies, Readmore, and Bennett's. We have seen Key merge into Ingram.

I concur with the predictions of John Secor and Len Schrift[17] — like the airlines, like department stores, like publishers themselves, only the strongest and the fittest vendors will survive until the 21st century. Those who do make it will be professionals committed to providing the highest levels of service with the greatest internal efficiencies and the lowest possible costs to clientele. They will assuredly be global in scope, multifaceted in services, and automated in all phases of business. They will be savvy and innovative marketers and dedicated and hard-working sellers. Their partnerships with both libraries and publishers will foster understanding of each sector. Because they survived the 1980's, even though battered and bruised, they are, ultimately, optimists, convinced that once again libraries will have money someday . . . and we'll go back to the good old days once again instead of just remembering them. They may have been knocked down, but they're not about to be knocked out.

NOTES

1. Kent Hendrickson, "Pricing from Three Perspectives: the Publisher, the Wholesaler, the Library," in *Pricing and Costs of Monographs and Serials: National and International Issues*, edited by Sul H. Lee, New York: The Haworth Press, 1987, p. 8.

2. See, for example, Ballen's Leonard Schrift, "Truth in Vending," in *Pricing and Costs of Monographs and Serials: National and International Issues*, edited by Sul H. Lee, New York: The Haworth Press, 1987, pp. 27-36 and Yankee Book Peddler's John R. Secor, "Scholarly Bookselling: An evolution in Progress," *Library Acquisitions: Practice and Theory* 12 (1988): 187-90, for cogent discussions of discounts, pricing, mix, and vendor expenses.

3. Schrift, "Truth in Vending," 31.

4. Secor, "Scholarly Bookselling," 188, and Schrift, "Truth in Vending," 33.

5. "New Scholarly Books," *The Chronicle of Higher Education*, 17 January 1990, A14.

6. Edna Laughrey, "Acquisitions Costs: How the Selection of a Purchasing Source Affects the Cost of Processing Materials," in *Pricing and Costs of Monographs and Serials: National and International Issues*, edited by Sul H. Lee, New York: The Haworth Press, 1987, pp. 53-66.

7. Ibid., 65.

8. Jonathan A. Lindsey, "Vendor Discounts to Libraries in a Consortium," *Library Acquisitions: Practice and Theory*, 5 (1981): 147-152.

9. Hendrickson, "Pricing from Three Perspectives," 11.

10. Leonard Schrift, "A period of Adjustment: Planning and Coping with Decreasing Funds in Libraries for Acquiring Monographs and Serials — a Vendor Perspective, *Journal of Library Administration* 10, no 1 (1989): 63-4.

11. Ibid., 63.

12. Ibid., 63-4, and Secor, "Scholarly Bookselling," 189-90.

13. Joseph W. Barker, "Library-to-vendor Electronic Order Transmission Today; Report of a Telephone Survey Conducted in December, 1988 for the Acquisitions Librarians/Vendors of Library Materials Discussion Group, *Library Acquisitions: Practice and Theory*, 13, no. 3 (1989): 276-7.

14. Ibid., 277.

15. Ibid., 279.

16. J. J. Walsdorf indicated that Blackwell North America receives 40% of its revenue from international accounts, *BP Report*, 19 February 1990, 6.

17. Schrift, "Truth in Vending," p. 33, and Secor, "Scholarly Bookselling: an Evolution in Progress," p. 188.

The Electronic Library: Analysis and Decentralization in Collection Decisions

Malcolm Getz

Electronic methods of storing, communicating, and manipulating information have had a dramatic effect in the libraries at Vanderbilt and we expect the drama to continue. If Vanderbilt's and other libraries are to take advantage of the new opportunities appropriately, libraries and their universities must assess the merits of the new information products. At the same time, libraries must reevaluate traditional practices. Should library budgets be larger to accommodate the new services? Will goals for building print collections change? Fortunately, the electronic systems also provide new tools for managing library services and should allow libraries to answer these questions with more information than has been possible in the past.

Let me first describe the electronic services in place at Vanderbilt. Vanderbilt has an innovative library and some of the services are unique. Second, let's talk about the reasons why some electronic services may be more valuable than print-based services. Third, let's discuss some analytic tools that can give new information to support collections decisions. Finally, let's consider the implications for collection goals.

THE ELECTRONIC SCENE AT VANDERBILT'S LIBRARY

Vanderbilt is a private university with 8,500 students, two-thirds of whom are undergraduates. Tuition in each of our ten schools is in

---

Malcolm Getz is Associate Provost for Information Services and Technology at Vanderbilt University, Nashville, TN.

© 1991 by The Haworth Press, Inc. All rights reserved.

excess of $12,000 so our clients expect extraordinary services. Vanderbilt is a major research university receiving over $90 million per year in research grants in medicine, engineering, sciences, and other fields. Vanderbilt competes with many other significant institutions for students, research grants, and institutional support. As a consequence, we seek to make careful investments that will enhance our ability to teach and study.

Vanderbilt's Library selected NOTIS in 1984 and implemented the public catalog in 1985 with circulation following early in 1986. By 1988, we had implemented all of the modules available in NOTIS. We began with a database of about 500,000 titles in OCLC, about two-thirds of our holdings. With OCLC's Microcon, we converted most of our holdings to electronic format by 1988. Our name for our local system is Acorn, a symbol from the University's shield. Acorn serves the eight libraries on campus. There are three technical processing centers: General, Law, and Medical and NOTIS supports them appropriately. The Acorn service is available over our campus broadband network, Caravan. We have invested in authority work on our bibliographic records and continue to invest in the revision of our database. Our core system has been very well received by our community. Novice users make comments like: "It doesn't seem like a computer." Experienced users make favorable comparisons with library automation systems they have used on other campuses.

In 1986, we received significant grant support from the Pew Charitable Trusts to extend our automation program in two directions. First, we installed twenty compact disk workstations and now subscribe to roughly fifty titles in compact disk format. We have article level indices in most of the disciplines of interest at Vanderbilt where compact disk products are available. Our Management Library makes aggressive use of compact disks with numerical and full-text information about businesses. Undergraduates now often teach one another to use the compact disks. In two locations, we have multiple compact disk servers serving multiple stations in the immediate vicinity, but compact disks are not yet on the campus network.

Second, with the Pew grant, we invited NOTIS to extend their software to support additional databases. Our librarians proposed

MedLine and three of the H.W. Wilson, Inc. databases as of sufficiently widespread interest to justify being mounted in the mainframe environment. Today, the most recent two years of MedLine, complete with Abstracts, and the Humanities Index, General Science Index, and Social Science Index from Wilson, are mounted as separate files in NOTIS. We are now adding the catalog of the Center for Research Libraries and a file of records for government documents. The user selects from these databases in a NOTIS menu in front of the book catalog, and can choose DPAC to get books, DMED to get MedLine, or DWIL to get the Wilson indices. These services went public in 1989 and usage is growing.

In 1989, Apple Computer gave Vanderbilt an equipment grant to develop a unique library service we call Clipper. We are scanning ephemeral material from vertical files at a reference station into electronic format on a Macintosh system. Optical character recognition software creates a character-based file from the scanned image. Users can conduct a keyword search of the full-text file and retrieve the scanned image. The search and delivery can be over the campus network to Macintosh systems. We are working on an HyperCard front-end to make end-user searching easier. We believe we are the first academic library to deliver full-page scanned images of documents over the network to end-users on demand.

Vanderbilt has made a significant commitment to electronic tools in the libraries. We are committed to delivering as much information as we can economically manage to users over our campus network. We prefer to use off-the-shelf software and components and will support a vendor in developing software in a direction of interest to us. Electronic tools are important to us. A number of other libraries are pursuing a similar agenda. We understand that nearly twenty other NOTIS libraries have already adopted the Multiple Database software.

WHY INVEST IN ELECTRONIC DOCUMENTS?

Electronic documents offer important advantages for libraries for four reasons. These reasons are sufficient to justify sacrificing other activities if necessary in order to develop electronic capabilities.

First, some documents are more valuable in electronic format than in any other. If a reader typically searches for a single entry in a long document as with an index to articles or a pharmacopoeia, the power of electronic searching makes the electronic version faster and more certain of success. For some documents, a searcher may be interested in establishing connections, word-associations, and interrelationships and the power of word searching will make an electronic version of the text more valuable. When numerical information is to be manipulated statistically and when any information is to be incorporated into a subsequent text, an electronic version will be more valuable because it can more easily be subjected to additional processing. Electronic documents can be dispatched over a network more easily and delivery to offices, dorms, and classrooms is significantly less expensive. For certain categories of documents, then, the electronic formats are significantly more valuable and will be worth a premium price over print. Book catalogs and article indices, many reference works, and full-text databases that are used piece-meal fall in this class.

We might note that journals have replaced books as the primary vehicle for communication in many disciplines because journals provide better access for scholars than books. Not only can ideas get to press more quickly with journals, but successful journals bypass the acquisition and cataloging operations of libraries. Just as journals have proved to be a superior technology to books, electronic documents will likely prove superior to journals in a number of disciplines. Access will be faster, and cumbersome, expensive library processes may be by-passed.

Second, some information is available only in electronic format. Certain government information and a number of numerical databases, surveys and electoral results are only available in electronic formats. If a library is to make these available to their constituencies, they must manage them electronically.

Third, the volume of print information continues to grow such that no library can acquire it all. In the mid-1980s, the world produced about 650,000 new titles per year.[1] The quantity of titles produced is strongly correlated with the rise of income or gross national product in many countries. If the world economy continues to grow as it has in recent decades, the world will likely produce one million new titles per year in the year 2000. Additionally, the advance of electronics has lowered the cost of producing printed material. The minimum quantity of volumes required by a publisher to break even on a new title has been falling. Now, McGraw-Hill publishes textbooks on demand, allowing adopting professors to select what will be in the book from a menu of material kept available at McGraw-Hill. We are approaching the time when an individual copy of a book can be tailor-made for a single purchaser.

A library will not be able to acquire all the printed books that are available or anything close to all. Electronic tools are then essential to locating materials over the national network and retrieving them on demand for a project at hand. Local electronic tools are effective ways of providing a window to a much larger world of information than any library can hope to accumulate within itself.

Finally, the costs of storage strongly lean toward increasing the amount of information that is stored electronically and decreasing the amount that is stored as conventional books. A typical book with character information contains about 2 megabytes of information. Table 1 shows that with a manufacturing cost plus storage space of over $20, a book has a storage cost in excess of $10,000 per gigabyte. Computer-output microfiche has a storage cost of about $1,500 per gigabyte. Write-Once Read Many (WORM) disks kept off-line have a storage cost of about $225 per gigabyte in small formats and as little as $60 per gigabyte in large formats. Robotic systems with WORM disks keep information on-line for about $500 per gigabyte. Very large scale robotic tape cartridge systems approach $200 per gigabyte. In short, to store large quantities of information, the storage costs of electronic system are much lower than print.[2] Moreover, technical changes in electronic storage should continue for another decade or longer and the tilt of costs in favor of electronic means of storage will become more and more pronounced.

The costs of electronic storage exhibit significant economies of scale. Large scale storage systems have lower costs per gigabyte than do smaller systems. Therefore, shared storage systems will likely be preferred to a wholly decentralized storage environment. Users of shared systems will also value cooperation in the organization and management of the shared information resources. Certainly

Table 1
Cost per Gigabyte of Storage Capacity
Representative Technologies

	Dimensions	Access	Unit Cost	Capacity in Gigabytes	Cost per Gigabyte
Book	500 pages	Off-line	$20.00	0.0020	$10,000.00
Microfiche	500 pages	Off-line	$25.00	0.1500	$166.67
small WORM Disk	off-line 5.25"	Off-line	$145.00	0.6500	$223.08
large WORM Disk	offline 12"	Off-line	$360.00	6.2000	$58.06
Floppy Magnetic Disk	3.5"	On-line	$505.00	0.0012	$420,833.33
Hard Magnetic Disk	microcomputer	On-line	$1,300.00	0.0400	$32,500.00
Hard Magnetic Disk	mainframe	On-line	$52,000.00	2.6000	$20,000.00
WORM Disk Robot	200 disks	robot	$600,000.00	1310.0000	$458.02
Magnetic Tape Robot	11000 cartrigdes	robot	$508,000.00	2420.0000	$209.92

an opportunity exists for library-like services based on electronic storage and a number of agents might provide such services.

For example, several vendors might present a full-text with graphics library of, say, 250,000 volumes on-line on the national network able to deliver full content on demand to end user workstations for a fee. The 250,000 volumes might include 5,000 current journals, the core of a reference collection, plus most of the books generally read by undergraduates. Of course, standards for storage and retrieval of complex documents must be established and arrangements made with owners of copyrights and these will take some time. However, the capital cost for a system storing a terabyte of data is well within reach of a number of organizations now and the costs will be lower than that of building and maintaining a print library of comparable scope. Moreover, for people with computers on a network, which most library users are, access to a remote electronic library via the network may be more convenient than access to the campus print library.

One can paint other scenarios as well. Disciplines are beginning to store draft working papers in electronic form and to distribute them over the network on demand rather than photocopying them and sending paper to colleagues. In time, each discipline may consolidate their service in a few repository centers, the centers will collect fees from both authors and readers, and working papers will become a more effective, faster, non-refereed vehicle for sharing research in progress.

Campus libraries will face new competition both from vendors on national networks and from other campus agencies in the management of electronic documents. Libraries, then, need to think carefully about what role is appropriate for them in the management of electronic information. What documents should be acquired for local mounting on high-speed magnetic devices, what should be kept on less expensive, but slower robotic systems, and what should be acquired in print? What documents should not be acquired locally but rather be fetched remotely via the network on demand? Fortunately, as the decision set becomes more complex, we will have some new tools to help.

ELECTRONIC MANAGEMENT TOOLS

Electronic systems can easily keep records that yield information that is relevant to managerial decisions, particularly collection decisions. In addition, some new electronic products are becoming available that already give a significant new dimension to collection policies.

The primary fact for an acquisition decision is the likelihood of use. With the more complex storage choices made possible by electronic systems, prediction of the likelihood of use will influence not only a decision about acquisition, but also choice of storage format. A document that is acquired but not used we call a Type II error, a false positive. A document that is not acquired but that would have been used we call a Type I error, a false negative. By systematically gathering information about patterns of use of similar material, we can make better forecasts about the likelihood of use of materials considered for future acquisition. With better forecasts, we can reduce the probability of both Type I and Type II errors, holding budgets constant.

A circulation system can generate reports on patterns of use by detailed call number category, by place of publication and language, and by date of publication. For the acquisition of print materials, this information can identify areas with significant amounts of Type II errors: books purchased but not used. For electronic documents, activity levels might be used to inform decisions about acquisition and mode of storage. More frequently used items can be maintained on higher speed storage devices, less frequently used items can be kept on less expensive devices.

Internal use of printed material in a library can be tracked as well. By scanning the barcodes on materials being reshelved, a library could track internal use and so have a broader base of information for forecasting use patterns, albeit at some extra cost.

Type I errors, materials not acquired that would have been used, might be identified in two ways. The brute force method is to examine transaction logs from search sessions so as to identify items that people search for but do not find. In today's environment, transaction logs are difficult to interpret. Too many non-hits are the result of spelling errors and search terms that are not recognized by the system. Once interfaces compensate for spelling errors and provide automatic cross references, transaction logs may yield information about Type I errors more easily. We might also wish to ask searchers to signal whether the item the system retrieves in fact looks appropriate to their needs. At present, we have no way of knowing whether a search hit actually meets the searcher's need.

OCLC has developed a new compact disk-based collection analysis tool that allows bibliographers to see local collecting results in light of the larger bibliographic universe.[3] At Vanderbilt, we call our program to see patterns in collections Argyle.

OCLC provides a compact disk with a brief bibliographic record for all of the monographic titles in the OCLC database published between 1978 and 1987 that are held by any academic member library, some 1.6 million recent monographs in all. Let's call this database the OCLC recent monographic universe.

OCLC defined several homogeneous groups of member libraries as peer groups: the largest quartile of members of the Association for Research Libraries (ARL), the second quartile in ARL, and a group of selective college libraries. Vanderbilt defined a group of peers for its own analysis as well. The OCLC collection analysis tool indicates how many members of each peer group hold each title and it indicates whether or not Vanderbilt holds the title.

An analyst can investigate a particular subject defined by an LC call number range, identify the number of titles in the universe for that subject, identify how many of the titles are held by, say, fifty percent of a given peer group (call these core titles), and then discover how many of the core titles are held by Vanderbilt. The average number of titles in the universe held by peers can be compared to the total number held at Vanderbilt. The system also indicates how many titles are held uniquely at Vanderbilt, and how many titles are held uniquely, on average, by each member of the peer group. The system provides lists of titles in subsets the analyst chooses (see Table 2).

An Argyle analysis then provides another approach to the problem of the Type I error: not buying material that would have proved useful. An Argyle analysis estimates the proportion of the biblio-

Table 2
Argyle: Patterns in Library Collections

An Example using the AMIGOS/OCLC Collection Analysis Compact Disk System

Peer Group is fifteen Research Libraries Choosen by Vanderbilt for Comparison
Counts are of monographs with Library of Congress catalog numbers held by an acedemic library
in OCLC published from 1978 to 1987.

column:		A	B	C	D	E	F	G
column ratios:				A/B		A/D		
		# of Titles Held by VU	All Titles among Peers	VU Holdings as ratio to total	Average # Held by Each Peer	Ratio: VU to Peer	Titles Unique at VU	titles Unique at Peer, avg

Subject by Call Number Range:

		A	B	C	D	E	F	G
E-F	History	6,580	26,949	0.244	6,426	1.024	410	871
F1201-1392	Mexican History	386	1,601	0.241	315	1.225	40	49
F1421-1577	Latin American History	473	1,743	0.271	374	1.265	10	36
F2201-3799	South American History	1,169	6,083	0.192	911	1.283	177	216
G	Geography	2,895	16,412	0.176	3,604	0.803	261	541
GN	Anthropology	931	3,547	0.262	1,097	0.849	28	84
GN700-875	Prehistoric Anthropolog	237	1,281	0.185	287	0.826	16	37

Detailed Subject by Call Number:

		A	B	C	D	E	F	G
F1219	Aztec History	170	422	0.403			19	
F1220-1331	Modern Mexican	32	103	0.311			1	
F1223-1235	Mexican History	120	537	0.223			10	
F1435	Mayan History	109	206	0.529			14	
F1465	Guatemalan History	22	80	0.275			1	
F3429-3430	Peruvian History	69	333	0.207			8	
GN803-845	European Archeaeology	40	212	0.189			5	

Note: The AMIGOS/OCLC System does not now easily produce reports about peer holdings for detailed classifications.

graphic universe being acquired and hints at the relative value of different titles in terms of the proportion of a significant group of libraries who have acquired it. To the extent that a library may wish to have maximized the usefulness of its collection in a field, it may aim to acquire a high proportion of core titles and avoid acquisition of other titles. Argyle gives an estimate of the success rate in achieving such a goal.

When a library aims to increase the research value of its collection, it will be concerned to increase the proportion of the bibliographic universe it is acquiring and to increase the number of unique titles in its collection. Argyle provides an estimate of a library's relative success in achieving such a goal. It can also provide an estimate of the budgetary commitment required to achieve particular objectives in given disciplines. Argyle analysis at one point in time can be used to set goals and refine budgetary allocations. Argyle analysis in subsequent years can reveal how well the goals are being met.

Library collection decisions, then, can be refined significantly in light of information generated as by-products of integrated electronic library management systems and by Argyle-style analysis. We will look for similar instruments to support decisions about serials, although such do not appear on the immediate horizon. Many electronic delivery services generate information about their use very readily, and decisions about commitments to electronic services should become easier as we develop a base of experience.

As decision support tools become widely used, we should expect decisions about collection goals to involve a wider circle of people and so to be decentralized in the organization. The analytic tools provide a vocabulary and an array of easily understood analysis that will allow deans and department chairs to review collection goals and to evaluate results. Such reports will come to play an important role in the self-assessments required in accreditation processes. As information about collection goals and results are more readily shared, the activity will become a more open process and, likely, a more decentralized process. Significantly sharper goals can be stated and achieved and library collecting efforts will more closely match the programmatic needs of the institution.

COLLECTION GOALS

The new environment should cause libraries to rethink their fundamental goals for collection building efforts and articulate the goals with significantly greater precision.

In the print world, the campus library was the only source of information for the campus community. Inter-library loan processes were too slow and cumbersome to account for more than a percent or so of the total use of library materials on a campus. Scholars whose needs were not well-served locally planned travel and leaves to visit other libraries with deeper or, at least complementary, collections.

Electronic services create new competition for conventional library services and a university's goals for its library will change as better electronic resources become available. For core collections, libraries will seek to support the local teaching program very well.

Competition will come from two sides. On the one hand, vendors will offer significant full-text resources directly to faculty and students via the network. The campus library must offer better services at reasonable cost to stay relevant.

On the other hand, individuals will have much greater storage capabilities on their desktops with personal compact disk drives and publishers offering compact disk libraries tailored specifically to particular markets: lawyers, surgeons, chemists, economists, and the like. Both IBM and Apple are likely to offer microcomputers with on-board CD drives aimed at multi-media communication, including compressed video, within a few years. When a CD or other optical drive with half a gigabyte or more of storage becomes a standard feature of personal computers, we should expect a blossoming of new information products that take advantage of the new delivery mechanism aimed at individuals. Such optical disks will move information in 2-300 volume chunks, a quite different scale than with print. The campus library will want to find economical ways to license and make available such compact disk products over the local network to students and to faculty in related disciplines.

The campus library will want to see its reserve room function and much of its reference service function delivered electronically via the campus network. The opportunity to tailor core services to the local scene gives the campus library an advantage, however, the service must be implemented at reasonable cost and with good quality.

However, as core services become more homogeneous across campuses, libraries serving research communities will seek to build distinctive collections. Universities will value world-class collections rich in unique materials on tightly focused themes. The collections will be valued for their comprehensiveness and for the quantities of original and unique materials. Significant electronic databases of full-text materials on an author, era, or genre, numerical databases, or databases on particular phenomena will feature as unique resources as well. The research collections can be thought of as collections in search of scholars. To some degree, such services may be offered to remote users via the national network, and we can expect the network to promote trade in access to unique information resources.

Collection goals will continue to be shaped by academic priorities: strong faculties build strong collections at least as much as strong collections attract strong faculties. Changing relative costs, however, will induce scholars to value a tilt toward electronic services with their higher retrieval speed, lower storage costs, and delivery to desktops via networks. Even as a significant suite of electronic documents is managed wholesale and as core collections become more homogenized, libraries also will develop very unique and highly specialized collections for use in trade via the national network.

SUMMARY

The challenge to library managers is clear. Electronic services are an important new opportunity that will cause us to rethink our mission and our markets. They will bring important new competition both via national networks and local desktops. At the same time, they will bring new tools that will allow libraries to manage their collections more aggressively. Most significantly, as electronic documents become more important, libraries will value tightly focused, comprehensive, world-class collections much more highly. In the history of the information age, we are still in the first ten seconds in a rapidly exploding universe. Libraries will not continue to hold a local monopoly on information resources, but well-managed libraries will find important and enduring roles.

NOTES

1. Malcolm Getz, "The Economics of Research Libraries: Present State and Future Prospects," *IFLA Journal,* vol. 15 (1989) no. 4, pp. 299-305.
2. Malcolm Getz, "Storage Technologies," *The Bottom Line,* vol. 4, no. 1, forthcoming, 1990.
3. AMIGOS markets the system for OCLC as "OCLC/AMIGOS Collection Analysis Compact Disk System."

J & B the Proper Blend: Harsh Reality or Seamless System

Charles Hamaker

In many ways, this talk is an opinion piece, informed by the perspective of a working acquisition and collection development librarian's seventeen some odd years going about the business of libraries.

The setting of course is less traditional than this statement implies because the last few years have forced on the academic library community the realization that traditional missions we have accepted can no longer be supported, even in theory. The gap between reality and theory has grown too large. The recent ARL statistics for 1988-89 bear out that overall, libraries are not doing what they believe they should be doing, and are not doing what they have believed was their mission. Many of you will have seen by now Graph 1 from the 1988-89 ARL statistics[1] ("Monograph and Serial Costs in ARL Libraries"). The drops in monograph acquisitions for ARL libraries in some instances are more severe than this graph suggests.

At LSU, for example, our situation is much worse, although volumes added are staying fairly constant due to large backlogs, both processed and unprocessed that are entering the workflow. We also have extensive exchange and gift programs which are holding volumes added at a fairly high level. But since 1985-86, with a static library materials budget, expenditures for monographs have dropped 59% (Graph 2 "LSU Libraries"). Almost every dollar of that drop comes from funds shifted to serials expenditures. After $200,000.00 in serials cancellations in the last two years, we

Charles Hamaker is Assistant Director for Collection Development at Louisiana State University, Baton Rouge, LA.

© 1991 by The Haworth Press, Inc. All rights reserved.

GRAPH 1. Monograph and Serial Costs in ARL Libraries (1985-86 – 1988-89)

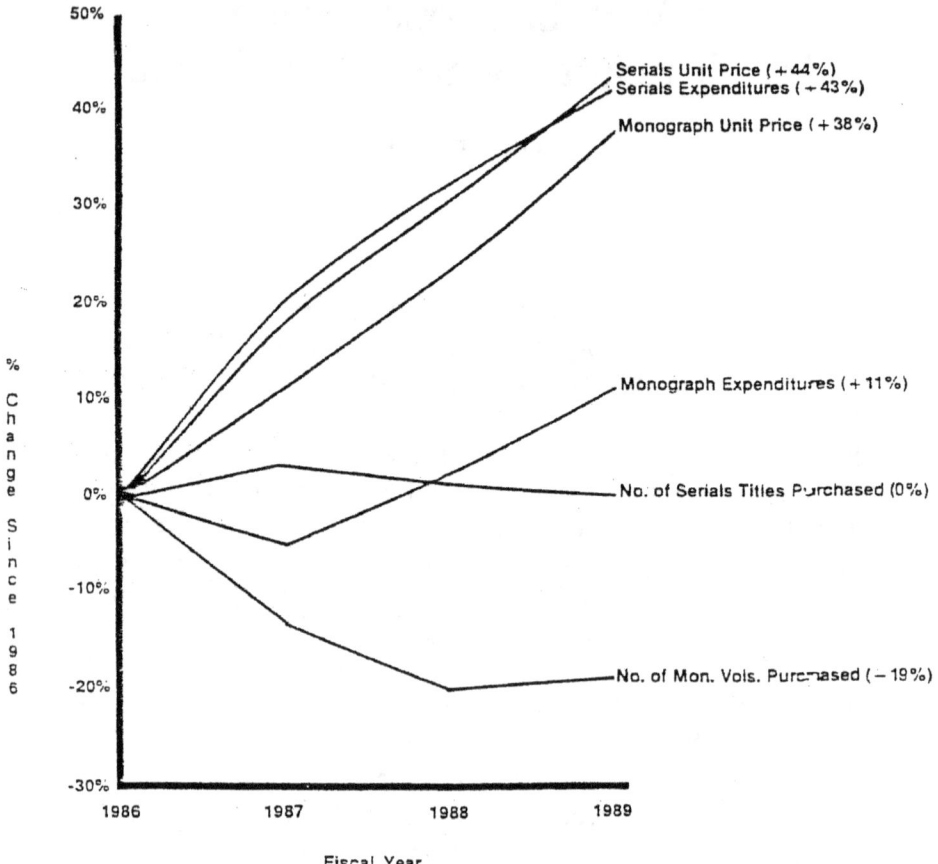

anticipate being able to hold our serials expenditures steady at last year's level of 1.6 million dollars.

The serials picture is old news by now but the problem is still with us. What both ARL and LSU's graphs show, that has not been discussed, is the level of increase in the unit price of books. For ARL libraries, a 38% increase in unit prices for books since 1985-86 is only five points off the 43% increase in serials expenditures.

While we were focusing on serials what happened to the price of books? To try and understand the dynamics in book pricing and to

GRAPH 2. LSU Libraries—Material Prices and Expenditures 1986-

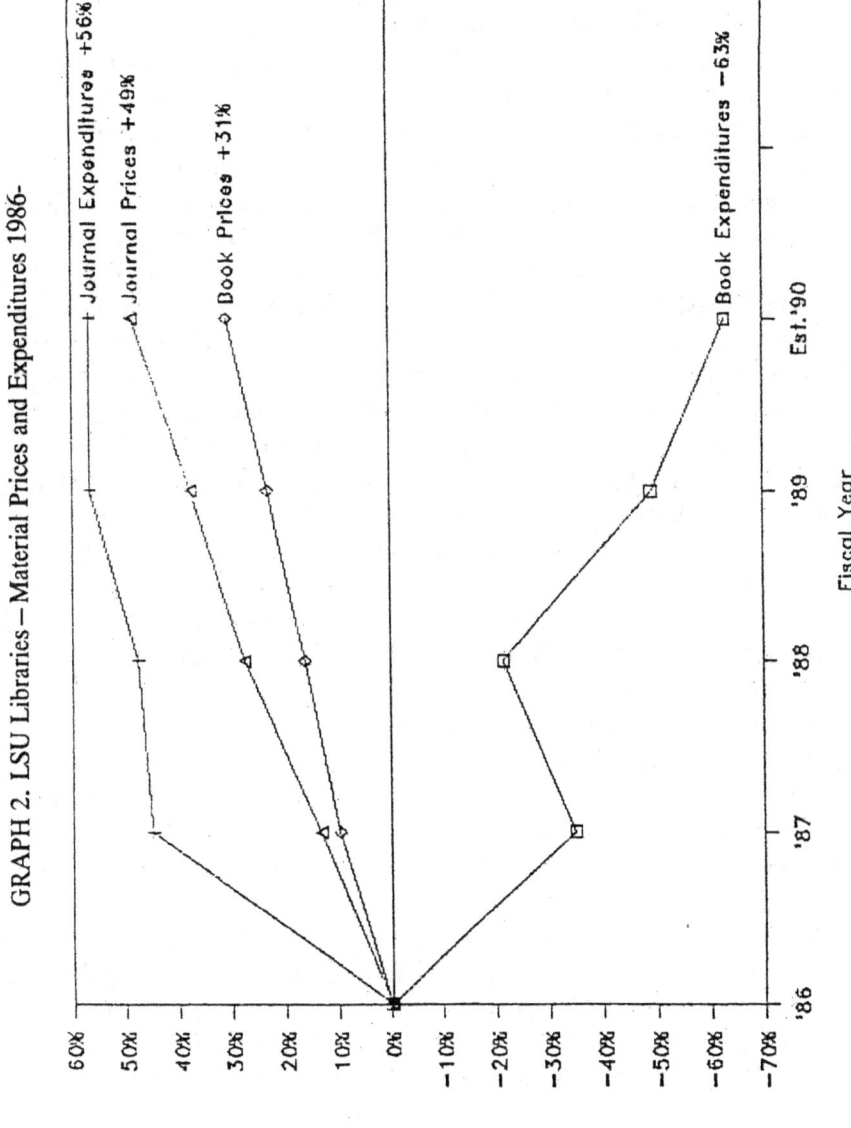

provide scenarios for steady state and growth budget projections for LSU for monographs, we went back to re-examine price and output data since 1984-85. We gathered data from the Baker and Taylor approval programs as a basis, although any comprehensive approval program statistics could have been used.

We were interested in two different aspects of the data. First, what was the cumulative effect of yearly price increases for academic books given the ARL figures. Second, and as important as the first, what had happened to title output. Both of these factors are significant, as libraries often express collecting goals as being a certain percentage of titles published in a particular subject area.

What we found was remarkably similar to the picture presented by Dana Alessi in an important talk she gave at the Oklahoma conference a few years ago, "Up the Elevator" which some of you here may remember. Because we couldn't add prices and titles directly, D.W. Schneider, our AD for public services and incidentally a librarian with an MBA, created an index for the two figures for each year. When those index numbers were combined, we had a figure which showed us how much, overall, a book budget would have to increase to maintain a constant proportional coverage of the literature (Proportional Literature Coverage Index, Graph 3). A second graph provided a look at how much we would have to increase our budget just to maintain a constant level of purchasing, i.e., the same number of books.

This next graph provides the percentage growth in price, percentage growth in title availability and the top line is a combination of these two figures with a 1984 base year (Graph 3, "Proportional Literature Coverage Index").

As you can see from Graph 4 (Serials and Monographs Average Prices-Index) which just looks at the percentage increase in average prices, that the lines overlap, confirming the ARL numbers. There is no difference in the two figures, which means that over the last five years, to remain constant in number of serials, and constant in number of books purchased, the same percentage increase would have had to be added to book budgets as was added to serials expenditures. These two systems with two different publishing decision sequences look identical in terms of the efforts needed to maintain comparable purchasing programs!

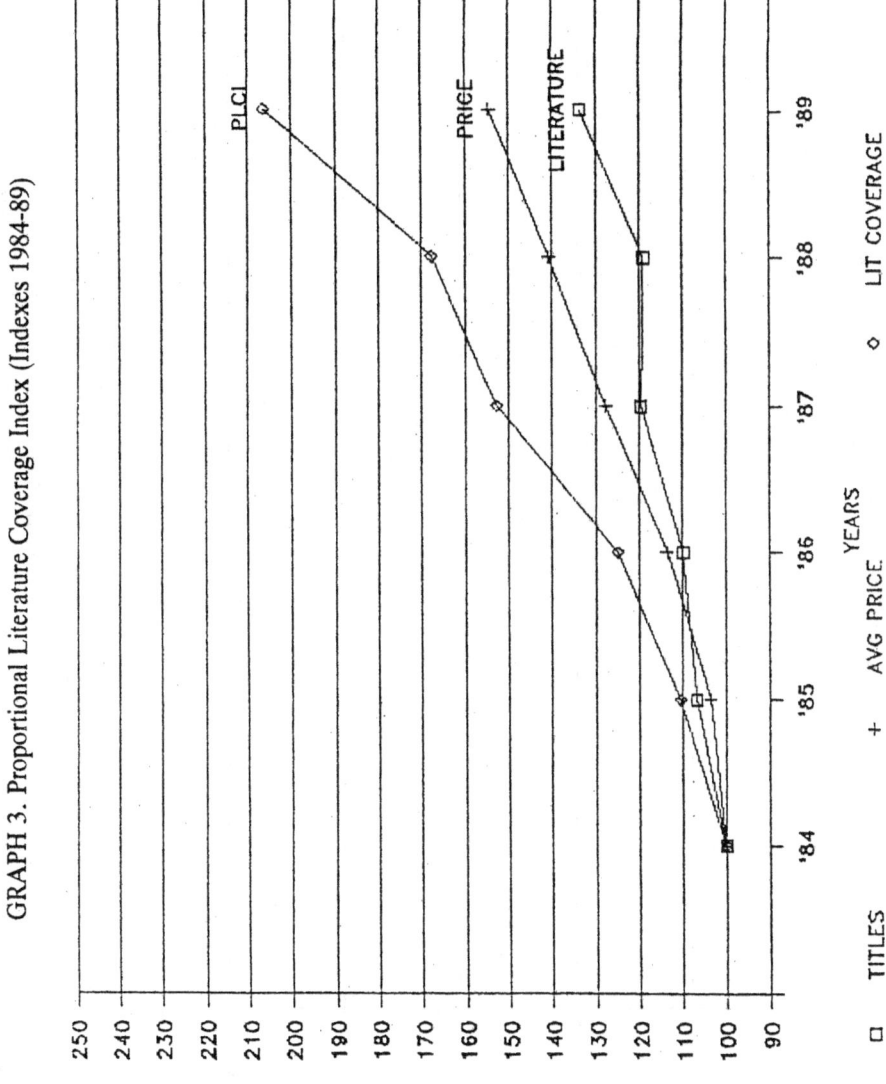

GRAPH 3. Proportional Literature Coverage Index (Indexes 1984-89)

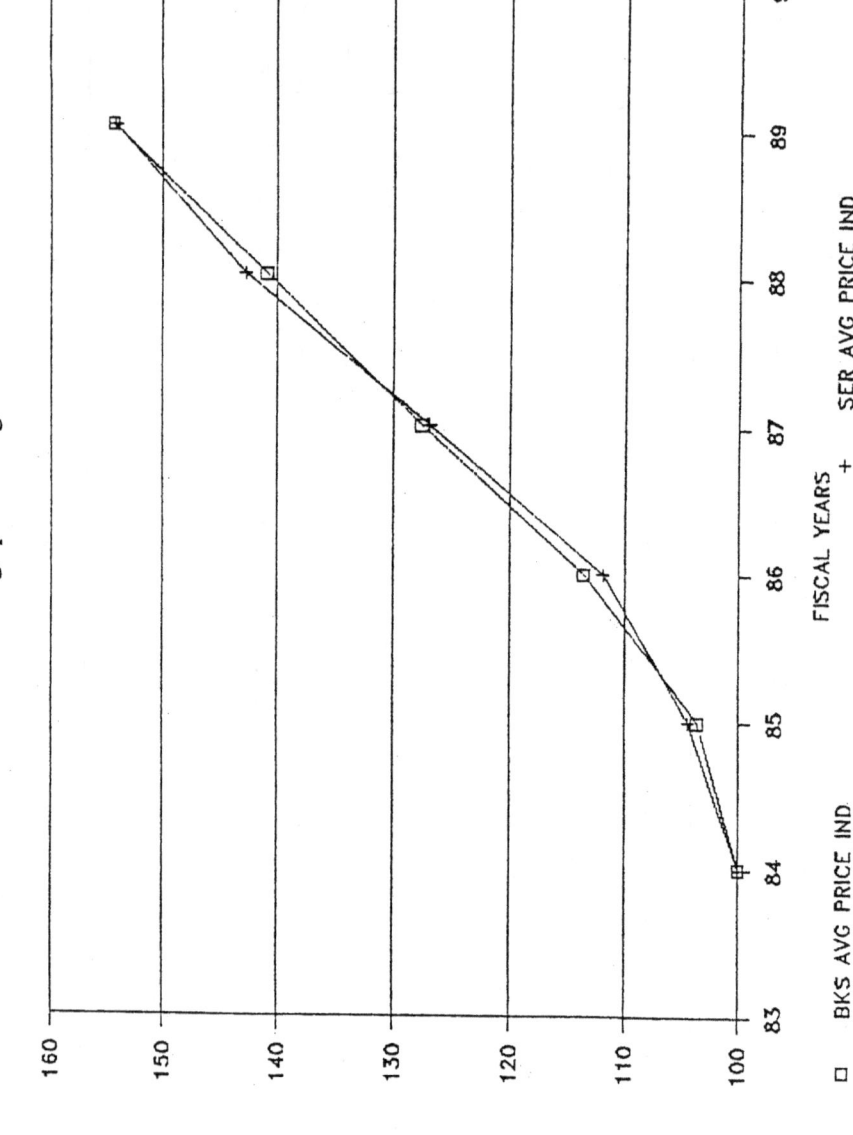

GRAPH 4. Serials and Monographs: Average Prices - Index

Because of this doppleganger effect we can no longer assume, if we ever did, that the forces pushing prices and output in journals are different from those creating pricing increases in books.

This finding and the lessons learned over the last few years "dialoging" about the serials system have led me to several personal conclusions. Because of new technologies, you will see as I continue that my ideas are beginning to suggest a clearer vision of the future. So here is my promised philosophizing and if you will pardon me, sermonizing:

I believe it is no longer sufficient for librarians to assume the basic context of their work is their own institution. There are only so many things you can do to contain the expenditure levels of a library for serials or monographs while still providing adequate access and coverage. Copyright limitation on access, for example, is an issue that cannot be addressed by librarians who believe their only responsibility is to decide what books or journals not to buy.

Contrary to publisher beliefs, the current situation is not a "library problem." It is a systemic problem. The answers to this "problem" as even publishers should have recognized by now, will not be found in the coffers of universities and colleges or of the federal government but through agreements and planning with faculty, with societies, and in the larger context with the institutions who provide the support that creates the current information system. That is where the power for change resides.

Librarians who have worked with OCLC or RLG over the last ten to fifteen years have long recognized that their local performance is intricately involved with national organizations. Not only shared cataloging but the modern interlibrary loan system are a direct product of activity and support forums external to local libraries.

Bibliographers, acquisitions and collection development librarians (much like serials librarians over the last four years) are beginning to realize the work they do for their institution must reach beyond institutional borders to be successful. This may include creating new ways of looking at standard pricing and output data. It may include new uses for the OCLC and RLG databases, which, if country of origin, format, date and subject categories were explored, as Anna Perrault and Beth Paskoff have demonstrated for Louisiana, could provide an extremely valuable overview of the health of America's libraries.[2] The Paskoff and Perrault study appearing in the April issue of *LRTS* (1990) provides "detailed information about the distribution of imprints according to age and language of publication, percentage of duplication, and distribution of serial and monographic formats in each subject section of the collection" (quote from the abstract). When examined by date of publication, the yearly profile indicates strengths and weaknesses as collections are effected by both budgets titles purchased and with external data added, title output. Monitored regularly such data could pinpoint problem areas in acquisitions nationally and provide indications of shifts in publishing patterns. It goes beyond either standard shelflist measurement techniques or the Conspectus in the level of detail and assessment, as the technique provides both detailed and verifiable data.

If inter-library cooperation, for all the many conferences and attempts to make it work has failed, then the logical question has become what else should we try. While collection development librarians have attempted over the last forty years to define collection interdependence as a workable concept the fact is quite simply that it has never really worked except in esoteric areas which have increasingly been divorced from the major costs of maintaining collections.

Alan Greenspan recently complained that an inflation level nationally of 4 1/2% was much too high. He has the tools to bring that down. Librarians, strapped with much higher increases in the cost of materials purchases for the better part of the last decade have had no effective means of controlling the "inflation" they have experienced. Increasingly we have recognized that publishers are the tender caretakers of our expenditures, and that particular machine seems to have its throttle stuck wide open.

The recognition that librarian participation in external forums may be critical to providing access to needed materials has led us to where there may in fact be real solutions—scientific and scholarly associations and societies and their members, the researchers of the world. Commercial publishers seem to believe that researcher commitments to them will override any concerns about the cost of access to information and the impact on research. This is the arena that librarians responsible for the care and feeding of collections are forced to enter for survival's sake.

Because Martin Gordon, for instance, or Herman Spruijt (of Elsevier) can scarce believe that Nobel laureates would deign to listen to librarians, that faculty could possibly pay attention to "clerks," they may believe the system of commercial scientific publishing, is still viable.

They have not recognized that at the end of day, the goals of researchers and teachers and librarians are closer than the goals of publishers and researchers. They believe that the inducements and prestige associated with their systems are more important to the individual than the good of the profession, of teaching, and of access to information.

It may come as a shock to them to learn that there is as much, commonality of interest between the Nobel laureate and the science librarian than ever existed between the publisher and the scientist. To explain to faculty members that a library now pours fifty percent more money into journals than in 1985-86 and has not been able to add a single new journal since that time is a message that will not go far from its mark—researcher behavior. A fundamental re-thinking of this system is beginning slowly but inexorably as researchers recognize their roles in maintaining a system that is causing the bronchial coughs of double pneumonia.

The AAAS annual meeting in New Orleans in February of 1990 included a panel chaired by Heinz Barschall. It was addressed by Fred Spillhaus of the American Geophysical Union, Dr. Robert Peet of the University of North Carolina-Chapel Hill and October Ivins of Louisiana State University. Advice from the scientific side of the table was revolutionary. Retake control of this publishing system before it is too late. Don't submit papers to overpriced, low quality journals. Don't let your name be used on the masthead of journals you have no control over. Be as ethical in this arena as you are in your own lab. If the system is out of control, it is scientists who have let it happen.

Bob Peet recommended reducing copyright coverage of STM articles to three years instead of the current system. Copyright, he asserted is an author right, not a publisher right. STM publishers believe it was created for them.³ (It was, in Queen Anne's day—our current laws vest original copyright in the author.)

Researchers know they didn't cause the problem, and they know librarians did not cause it either. That's the perspective seen all over the world in various guises—wherever publishers depend on the goodwill of scholars for both the "supply" and "demand" side of a tidy, profitable equation, and libraries to pay the bills. Even in the humanities and liberal arts, scholars are asking why a book from Cambridge University Press is so expensive they can't afford to buy copies of their own work.

At times it seems as if certain publishers are bent on self destruction: the pure greed (and in some instances delight) of British publishers charging American libraries double what they charged other libraries for some titles worldwide; the unalloyed profiteering of some commercial publishers that may average four to five times prices that associations set in terms of both pages and words delivered. These are not mere artifacts of the system, but tools making fortunes and point clearly to what is destroying it as surely as the so called "glut" of publishable quality papers.

Who are libraries' natural allies? That is the basic question for librarians looking for ways to find control mechanisms as powerful as those at Alan Greenspan's disposal. With no reserve board controlling the flow of papers, what changes are needed to create a system that will promote the availability of the basic product used in our libraries—information in its various forms and shapes. Depend on the market place is a slogan some would have us adopt. That's a nice slogan, but the system runs on a monopoly basis (protected by government) and has developed strong tendencies (as Dick Dougherty has reminded us) towards oligopoly. In addition, new technologies have helped clever publishers to learn how to make a profit on journals or on books selling a few hundred copies; that is, only publishing what very few people actually need or want and charging such a price for it that what more people do want, but don't have the political clout to demand—cannot be purchased.

The most current example, lest we forget, is the incredible prices publishers, both commercial and society, believe they should charge for CD-ROM products. This supposed revolution in distributing information is being priced out of the reach of the common user, and out of the reach of many libraries, especially in research information areas. At a reproduction cost of two dollars a disk, publishers have shifted gears to tell us how 90% of *their* cost is "independent" of the medium of distribution. Instead of looking at the characteristics and potentials of the medium, publishers are attempting to replicate incomes from the paper form in electronic media at the very beginning of its life cycle. This approach is errant nonsense.

In addition, because society won't talk with society, nor publisher with publisher, the standardization that could make the potentials of this new media available world-wide are not being developed fully. And the current pricing schemes aimed at recovering development costs quickly, ignore the fact that libraries provided the money for those development costs in the first place.

A major sign of faith in the very information they claim to exist to support is long overdue. By creating cost structures that accelerate and increase access to the resources being reformatted, publishers could prove they believe in what they are doing. The cynical pricing of Compact Disk products is proof the tiger has not changed its stripes.

Look at the need for information in the third world, in Africa, in Mexico, even many libraries in the U.S. — and the potential that now exists — plan for a future of unlimited access, not pay per peek access. Stop trying to perpetuate the same old game, more money for less product and less distribution — in the new medium.

The bottom line is not how soon can the product recover development costs, but how can this new media be used to do what the old media has proven incapable of doing. Widespread distribution AND profit. Forget the carriage without the horse.

Evidence of using this new media to increase sales and thus distribution is lacking not only in commercial products, but in NLM products, commercial re-workings of census bureau data, databases created to support print products, and what few full-text products are available. Profitability is one question, sustainability and accessibility is the larger question. If the larger question is answered, the first question will answer itself.

I believe that if it is not answered successfully by commercial producers, it will be answered by the institutions whose very lifeblood is access and distribution of information—academia and their libraries. If you doubt it can be done, re-examine the extensive exchange systems in place before, after and during World War II. With cheap duplication on CD-ROM a viable product, it is only a matter of time before Academies world-wide recognize that the responsibility for dissemination of information is now an economically viable proposition. At LSU our entire exchange program could be handled by CD-ROM for essentially the same price we now pay for all of the materials we send on exchange, and we could more than quadruple the volume. The capability now exists to give the world access to the research created on our campuses—economically.

Cleveland Public Library's proposal to convert serial backfiles to CD-ROM was something an AAP-CCC task force "refused to consider at this time." Frances Clark, the public relations director at Cleveland Public says that the library has the capability for this conversion now. How long will institutions whose primary missions are research, dissemination and service permit the current stalemate to continue when new technologies promise assistance in all three areas?[4]

Copyright, which has been essentially a publisher right as practiced since its introduction in Queen Anne's 1710 act, may finally become a real author or producer right because of new distribution capabilities. By statute it belongs to author as creator—not publisher as distributor. The author's goals, not the publisher's, may rapidly become the primary criteria for publication in STM fields. For publishers, the word from libraries and their institutions is provide inexpensive access or face an even more limited role in the world-wide information system than you presently have.[5]

Librarians moving out of libraries to work in the larger context of the information system generally have a uniform ethical stance toward the free flow of information. GODORT's view is in fact almost universal in the library community. DTTP. We are populists. Information, ultimately, is for the good of the community. Publishers will either join actively and creatively in enhancing the process, or face becoming dinosaurs collapsing under the weight of their own overhead. Even in the name of "capitalism"—which in fact is a monopoly system in this instance, they won't be permitted to take the whole system with them. Public good is, in the STM fields, at least as important, and perhaps more so than publisher's rights. Author's needs and goals drive the system. As their goals diverge from the commercial publisher's, the new technologies promise to put authors and their institutions even more in the driver's seat.

I hope I have provided enough evidence and conjecture to show that librarians must move out of the library if we are going to be successful in providing for the future of our institutions. Not only that, we must communicate what we find as we look outside, and work towards a commonality of interests and philosophy, while actively exploring a variety of approaches. One of the most glaring deficiencies in ALA, ARL and all the other alphabet soup of organizations right now is the lack of a real agenda for dealing with the "library" problem. Surely with all the talks and studies that have been conducted in the last few years, we should be near producing a working agenda for the profession and for others concerned with the same problems. The lack of that agenda is part of what has perpetuated the current crisis. And the lack of leadership which is symptomatic of the profession in this area may well be a result of our insular vision back home "on the ranch." It's time to step out and explore possibilities in the wider world.

NOTES

1. *ARL Statistics 1988-89* (Washington D.C.: Association of Research Libraries, 1990) p. 6.

2. For an example of how this data could be viewed, see Beth M. Paskoff and Anna H. Perrault "A Tool for Comparative Collection Analysis: Conducting a Shelflist Sample to Construct a Collection Profile" *LRTS* (April, 1990) forthcoming issue as of the date of this talk. Their study has been extended to most of the academic libraries in Louisiana and on University of California campus.

3. See Spillhaus and Peet comments in Kim A. McDonald "Scientists Urged to Help Resolve Library 'Crisis' by Shunning High-Cost, Low Quality Journals" *Chronicle of Higher Education* (Feb. 28, 1990) p. A13.

4. See Frances Clarks comments in Gary Handman, "Textbook Publishers Ponder an "Information Age" *Library Journal* (Feb. 15, 1990) pp. 146-147.

5. For a fascinating discussion of copyright history and possible directions, see Kanwal Puri "The Term of Copyright Protection: Is It Too Long in the Wake of New Technologies." *UNESCO'S Copyright Bulletin* xxxiii (3) 19-32.

Who Gets What: Allocating the Library's Materials Budget

Robert L. Houbeck, Jr.

While reading to my children recently I came across the following passage from Mark Twain's *Adventures of Tom Sawyer*, and I was struck by its applicability to our topic today. Some of you may recall the scene. Tom is displaying to an admiring crowd the tooth he had recently pulled when Huck, not to be outdone, displays an equally enticing novelty: a wood tick that he has been keeping in a small box. Working up to a swap, the two rivals begin a cautious circling ritual:

"Say, what's that?"
"Nothing but a tick."
"Where'd you get him?"
"Out in the woods."
"What'll you take for him?"
"I don't know. I don't want to sell him."
"All right. It's a mighty small tick anyway."
"Oh, anybody can run a tick down that don't belong to them. I'm satisfied with it. It's a good enough tick for me."
"Sho, there's ticks aplenty. I could have a thousand of 'em if I wanted to."
"Well, why don't you? Becuz you know mighty well you can't. This is a pretty early tick, I reckon. It's the first one I've seen this year."

Robert L. Houbeck, Jr. is Head, Acquisitions & Serials Divisions, the University of Michigan Library, Ann Arbor, MI.

© 1991 by The Haworth Press, Inc. All rights reserved.

> "Say, Huck—I'll give you my tooth for him."
> "Less see it."
> Tom got out a bit of paper and carefully unrolled it. Huckleberry viewed it wistfully. The temptation was very strong. At last he said:
> "Is it genuwyne?"
> Tom lifted his lip and showed the vacancy.
> "Well, all right," said Huckleberry, "it's a trade."
> Tom enclosed the tick in the percussion-cap box that had lately been the pinchbug's prison, and the boys separated, each feeling wealthier than before.[1]

Each feeling wealthier than before. What Mark Twain has done here, of course, is describe precisely and memorably the essence of the market, the free exchange of resources for assets, with each participant feeling enriched by the transaction. As economist Paul McCracken remarked to me when I drew this passage to his attention, Adam Smith couldn't have said it better.

The problem that has occupied so much of our attention in recent years, and which brings us together these two days, is our sense that something has gone wrong with the market in which libraries act. Increasingly, for example, many of us have had to rob our monograph budgets to support an ever expanding list of key journal titles, never mind freeing up money for the purchase of new electronic formats. Increasingly, some of the prices asked seem too dear and leave us with too few teeth to swap for ever more ticks.

I don't plan to focus today on the question of just what it is that is wrong with that market in which libraries transact business. What I'd like to talk about, rather, is how we deal with some of the consequences of that shortfall in teeth and ticks. First, I'll focus on a budget management technique we put into place at Michigan several years ago which has enabled us to keep some balance between our serial and monograph acquisitions. But, since what I'll be describing is really only a coping technique, I also want to discuss some ideas for expanding our materials budgets. Toward that end, sandwiched in the middle, I'll indicate some of the trends that will condition that search for new funding. I am, of course, in this paper speaking only as a professional librarian to his colleagues, not as a representative of my particular institution.

As I was putting together these remarks a few weeks ago, I received the latest issue of Marcia Tuttle's *Serials pricing newsletter*.[2] One of the articles described the problem confronting a major East Coast research library. This library has not had a materials budget increase in three years. Monograph acquisitions have dropped 40%. Though they have been steadily cancelling serials, they find that they must now engage in yet another major cancellation round. Those are brutal numbers: no new funds for three years, 40% fewer monograph acquisitions, and additional serial cuts. Reading her description, I did not regret the title I had chosen for this discussion: Who gets what. It is, of course, part of the ungentle subtitle of Harold Lasswell's book, *Politics*. In the light of such numbers, my title, if crude, seems entirely apt to our subject.

One of the key insights from Harold Geneen's book, *Managing*,[3] is the admonition: "Managers must manage." Now, the former longtime executive officer of ITT meant several things by this phrase, but chief among them was the insistence that his managers had to solve problems and solve them with the resources available. Over the last two decades, the shape of many libraries' materials budgets has been turned completely around. Where in 1967 academic libraries spent, on average, just 20% of their budgets on journals, today many are spending 70% and more.[4] Accompanying this shift have been steep declines in the number of monographs acquired by libraries.[5] So, in this first section, let me describe briefly a key technique we have used at Michigan that has enabled us to keep some control over our serial/monograph collection pattern.

Like many research libraries, Michigan has by tradition divided its materials budget into subject- and language-related funds. This division, into some 130 funds, has at least the sanction of custom. Apart from a large general serials fund for the main humanities and social sciences collection, however, we did not, until a few years ago, subdivide those funds into monograph and serial (or what we have come to refer to as continuing and non-continuing) subfunds. By the early-1980s, we began to feel the need for more detailed budget management data. The Innovacq acquisitions system, which we purchased in 1983, provided us with the tool and the occasion to enhance that control.

Foreseeing the analytical power of the Innovacq software and anticipating the need for more highly differentiated information about our expenditures, Dick Dougherty, our then-Director, had each of our several dozen fund managers subdivide their funds between "continuing" and "non-continuing" purchases. But in addition to such apportioning, he asked each to set an ideal ceiling above which their serial expenditures should not rise. So, for example, our physics fund manager might have allocated 75% of his budget for the purchase of physics serials but also set a ceiling of 85% for that type of material. He wanted, that is, to always retain at least 15% of his budget for monographs. For his particular collection and patrons, that serial/monograph mix seemed best. What we put in place for each subject area, then, based on our judgment of campus needs, was a cap on the percent our serial expenditures could consume.

Those ceilings proved invaluable when, a few years later, the dollar fell abruptly and foreign serials accelerated in price. We had in place both the analytical software and the allocation mechanism to enable us to manage our budget during a period of real crisis. For the past several years, then, when a fund has hit the allocation ceiling for continuing expenditures, that fund manager has had to identify titles for cancellation—or make a convincing argument that patron demand for serials in that discipline has so changed that a higher ceiling is warranted.

Has this system worked? Yes. Our objective was to keep our expenditures for continuations at or below 55% of our total materials allocation. Over the last four years, the percentage of continuations expenditures has ranged from 52-55%. Mission accomplished.

Two additional factors—aside, of course, from Providence—also helped. First, we kept in the first few years roughly 6-8% of our budget in an unallocated fund, which we could use at discretion to tide-over with onetime money subject funds that were especially hard-hit by unanticipated inflation. And second—and here's where we have really been fortunate—the Library's materials budget has continued to occupy a very high priority on the University's agenda. Relative to other campus units, we have received extremely generous support. While we have had to cancel titles, we had to cancel far fewer than would have been the case had we occupied a lower place at table. There really is no substitute for that kind of support. Our challenge will be to maintain that support, which is a topic I want to return to later.

What I've described in this first section is not particularly revolutionary. Many of you may have in place similar mechanisms—though my conversations over the last few months with colleagues around the country suggest that there are still lots of places that do not have such controls in place.

But the problem, of course, is that ceiling-setting is really only a coping technique. It helps you keep the pie sliced in what is for your institution the right proportions; but it doesn't get you a bigger pie. To get a bigger pie, you have to pick more apples.

Now a lady who may or may not know much about baking pies but who surely knows how to supply other grandmothers with more apples once remarked with a fine tartness: "No one would have remembered the Good Samaritan if he had only good intentions. He also had money."[6] Money is what this conference is about—how to get more of it to realize those good intentions that are at the heart of our mission: to support the research, teaching, and educational needs of faculty and students, today and in the future. We accomplish that mission by expending resources to acquire assets, ticks for teeth, some of which we buy outright, others of which we merely rent.

Some of you may recall the perhaps apocryphal exchange between Alfred North Whitehead and someone who was probably an administrator: "You know, Professor Whitehead, one could burn half the books in the British Museum, and no one would know the difference." To which Whitehead casually inquired: "Which half?"

That anecdote describes concisely one of the key challenges confronting research libraries. Indeed, twenty percent of our collections may serve eighty percent of our users quite well. But research collections exist to serve not only the mass but also, and perhaps even primarily, the margins. With the twigging of disciplines that is the result of increased specialization, those margins are expanding.

As the Whitehead quip cautions, it is probably not possible to know at the front end with any very great precision which half of new published material will be needed or will prove fruitful for researchers. So after selectors have done their best to winnow, in the end the preeminent research libraries have been those whose universities have spent the most on building broad and deep collections.

But we all know that appetites are bottomless. Some of you will recall that *College & Research Libraries* recently republished a 1968 article that might have been written last month: "The Bottomless Pit, or the Academic Library as Viewed from the Administration Building."[7] The human reality is that no one ever believes that his budget is adequate. But the plaintive, "How much is enough?" asked by every university administrator of every library director has to be answered with another question: "What sort of library collection do you want?" "What institutional objectives do you want the library to fulfill?" The answer to those questions always will be related in part to the mission of the library and the ambition of the campus and in part to the competition for resources within the institution as well as the competition for students, faculty, and status between institutions. What are your institutional objectives? What do your faculty expect? What are your peers, your competitors, willing to deliver?

An analog, also in the publicly funded sphere, is the defense budget. "How much is enough for defense?" It's not a question that can be answered in the abstract or by formula. The level of defense spending is based on a dynamic assessment of the capabilities of potential opponents. The concept of "enough" means "enough to achieve our policy objectives." The measures of success in defense, too, are as vague but as real—if perhaps more critical—as in the level of library funding. You are successful if you are strong enough to deter an opponent from even starting a conflict or, as seems now to be the case in Eastern Europe, if your level of spending was sufficient to reduce the threat by forcing your opponent into peaceful internal reforms.

Now, clever bureaucrats can always construct clever arguments in support of a new weapons system or an augmented materials budget. The key, though, is to persuade the people who control the money to make your priority their priority. Before turning to that process of persuasion, let's spend some time considering a few key internal and external trends within the higher education information system that will form the context for administrative decision-making over the next several years.

First, there will continue to be more books to buy than any of us can afford.[8] (Similarly with printed journals.)[9] The library as a place which houses printed materials will not be rendered obsolete next year. Compared to electronic formats, print is still cheap, convenient, familiar, and the preferred medium for published scholarly communication in the great majority of disciplines, including many of the sciences. For those of us in research libraries, whose business it is to collect the material at the margins—the publications of small research institutes, of out-of-the-mainstream publishers, of the constellation of large and small interest groups that is the trial and the glory of a pluralist society—the documents produced by these groups, we can be sure, will not soon be issued on CD. If we want them, we'll have to buy them in print.

Those of us whose universities support programs in Eastern European and Soviet studies also will be confronted with an explosion in newly available and newly revised printed material, an expansion similar to that of the last few years in China. We might expect, too, though this is more speculative, that more and more material will be issued in English, partly to foster communication with the West but more importantly to provide hard currency to impoverished economies.[10] Acquisition of this material will demand new money, and certainly it will be available only in print format.

Over the next several years publication in electronic formats will continue to expand in reference materials and perhaps in the area of the low-circulation, no-advertising scholarly journal. Already many reference sources are produced in CD formats. And one can understand why. They lend themselves well to electronic technology: they are consulted rather than read, can be easily and frequently updated, and use is known to be heavy. They have, that is, stable, predictable markets. Large-scale electronic distribution of journals, however, though seemingly ideal products for such a mode of distribution, is not yet in place for a combination of reasons. The latest edition of ULRICH's lists 2,100 journals as available online. Most of those titles, however, can hardly be said to be online journals.

What is available is text, few tables, and no graphics. Technological limitations are not the primary impediment to expanded marketing of these products in electronic formats. In many disciplines, authors and faculty users are not yet demanding publication in such formats. I would expect the professional associations to approach electronic distribution very cautiously. Commercial publishers, for their part, have as yet no economic incentives to offer in electronic format for their large circulation journals, which are supported mainly by individual subscribers and advertising. Even their small circulation research journals, despite diminishing subscriptions, are still steady, relatively predictable sources of up-front revenue. Until copyright, pricing, and downloading issues are resolved, I would not expect to see publishers eager to release enhanced, print-quality products into a network environment. Copyright and related intellectual property issues, in fact, are likely in the next decade to be one of the key battlegrounds between the often overlapping interest groups that form the academic information distribution chain of producers, distributors, and consumers.[11]

An as yet unknown variable in the distribution of research is the developing academic communications networks. Certainly, networks such as BITNET and INTERNET have greatly enhanced the ability of scholars across the nation to communicate and exchange data.[12] The National Science Foundations' computer network, NSFNET, whose operations center is located at my own University, has, in fact, been described as "the academic equivalent of the interstate system."[13] The numbers certainly support that image. Two-hundred thousand micros are tapped into this roadway, a conduit linking "six supercomputer centers, nineteen midlevel networks, over 1,000 university and commercial research centers nationwide, and nearly a dozen computer networks abroad."[14] Traffic over NSFNET during December 1989 amounted to the equivalent of half a *billion* typed, double-spaced pages, an increase of 550% over December 1988. (To place that figure in perspective, Elsevier, the world's largest commercial publisher of scientific and technical information and long-established in the information trade, produces 775,000 printed pages per year.)[15]

The development of NSFNET exemplifies another key trend within higher education: increasingly close cooperation between universities and the private sector. Michigan's Vice Provost for Information Technology, Doug Van Houweling, recognizing that the University would need partners if its bid for the NSFNET operations center were to be successful, evangelized IBM to the tune of $45 million for computer hardware and network design and MCI for $10 million in long-distance service.[16] IBM and MCI saw investment in the system as an opportunity to test new hardware and as an internal communications vehicle for their own extensive R&D staff.

There are other examples of increased cooperation between industry and the academy, such as the proposal currently before Congress to fund a National Research and Education Network. A few additional from my own University are as follows: twenty-five miles of fiber optic cables from Northern Telecom, worth $1 million; another project with IBM, called the Institutional File System (IFS) Project, designed to enhance data-sharing across campus by enabling users to share data produced on normally incompatible systems. "The IFS system," Van Houweling observes, "could serve as the prototype for a worldwide electronic library accessible from any type of computer."[17]

Or listen to the Vice Provost speak about UMI, which is also located in Ann Arbor. "Not a lot of people know it, but UMI turns out to be one of the largest information storehouses in the world. They have almost all the dissertations and theses that have been written in the United States. They now routinely microfilm almost all of the major publications in the world, including the major newspapers. For the last fourteen years, they've been doing that at a level of quality that means a computer can actually scan that microfilm and put it in machine-readable form. So, we've started discussions with UMI about ways to work together with them."[18]

I've spent time on these examples and quotes because they seem to me of far more than local interest. They portend, I believe, explicitly and between the lines, major changes in library service in the developing academic information infrastructure. "Universities," Van Houweling notes, "are basically in the information business. We're absolutely dependent on timely access to information, both for teaching and research."[19] Those are words from a Vice Provost that librarians would do well to ponder.

Another reason, of course, that universities are pressing forward with the application of these new technologies, is the heightened competition among them for faculty and students. Part of the motivation for this competition is demographic. That portion of the population between 18 and 24 years of age has been declining and will continue to decline for the next decade. Contrary to predictions, enrollments have continued to climb slowly.[20] Still, it is likely we will very soon see a leveling off and perhaps an actual decline in college admissions, lasting at least into the mid-90s. So, administrators are intent upon providing this steady or shrinking base of customers with a more attractive product.

There is also heightened competition for quality faculty, where quality is defined by both the ability to attract grant funding and by output of research. But in order to secure those grants and publish that research, faculty need facilities and rapid information delivery and manipulation technologies. The pressure on available research funding is intense. The percent of national R&D money contributed by the private sector, though still a small percentage of the total, has doubled in the period 1972-87. The contribution of foundations has increased by 50%. Nor has Federal funding over the period lagged behind, increasing, in constant dollars, by 63%.[21] The NIH budget, for example, in just the last decade, grew by 50%, in constant dollars.[22] Yet, despite these increases, NIH in 1989 was able to fund just 29% of all approved projects, an all-time low. Even with steady increases in base funding well in excess of inflation, only about one in four new projects actually receives funding.[23] The competition is fierce and universities find that they must provide their productive faculty with the best and latest tools, or they will jump to those places that will. My own University's R & D Division has just opened an office in Washington precisely to have people close to the funding agencies alert for shifts in emphasis, criteria, and direction. Every research university will be looking for a similar leg up on the competition.

An acquaintance recently remarked how, before entering the academy, he had envisioned a future in which he would spend his days strolling over tranquil, wooded campuses chatting amiably with colleagues about medieval metaphysics. Instead, behind the manicured ivy and twenties neo-Gothic, he found, as we all have, that college campuses are as nasty and brutish, and occasionally decent, as any other space inhabited by unredeemed mortals. They are places in which people compete for resources and recognition and in which there never seems to be enough of either — the garden after the apple.

Indeed, within universities, too, as we know all too well, there is increased competition for resources. Nationally, it is not a battle libraries are winning. Consider the chart,[24] put together by the Department of Education's National Center for Education Statistics (see Table 1). The table describes the relative growth, in constant dollars, of expenditures over the last decade at public institutions of higher education. You'll note that, at universities, in 1986 (the latest year for which figures are available) funding for libraries has grown at the lowest pace of any of the seven categories measured. Among four-year institutions, only expenditures on scholarships lagged behind library funding. The chart for private institutions reveals similar numbers. While there are always a variety of ways in which to interpret statistical tables, the trend lines for libraries do not look encouraging. For whatever reason, we are not keeping pace in the internal competition for funds. And when you start to fall behind on the priority chart of your institution, there is trouble around the bend.

These trends are formidable — more print materials, more materials issued in electronic formats, more competition among universities, more internal competition for funding, a growing undertone of questions about the role of libraries in an increasingly wired environment. In the words of the well-known Russian phrase, "What is to be done?"

What is to be done, it seems to me, is to stand and fight. But fighting, in the overtly genteel venue of the academy, means finding the right levers and the right language.

The funding sources open to us are internal and, to a much lesser extent, external, and we should be cultivating both. Here is a flavor of what I mean by levers and language.

Too often libraries are seen, at least by administrators, as black holes into which dollars pour. But we are more than opaque boxes collecting expensive square paper packages. What we need to do is to find ways to open up those packages more widely than ever, to

Indicator 2:13

Table 2:13–1 Index of expenditures in constant dollars per full-time-equivalent student at *public* institutions of higher education, by type of institution: Academic years ending 1977–1986

(1977 = 100)

Year	Total	Educational and general expenditures [1]						
		Instruction	Administration [2]	Research	Libraries	Public service	Operation and plant maintenance	Scholarships and fellowships
				Universities				
1977	100	100	100	100	100	100	100	100
1978	101	102	103	102	96	98	102	96
1979	103	103	104	106	94	103	105	90
1980	99	98	96	105	103	98	99	86
1981	96	95	96	103	89	99	96	85
1982	96	95	97	100	88	96	98	83
1983	97	97	98	102	91	97	101	85
1984	101	100	102	105	96	100	104	91
1985	107	105	112	114	98	106	109	96
1986	114	110	120	122	104	113	110	107

					Other 4-year institutions			
1977	100	100	100	100	100	100	100	100
1978	101	101	102	102	100	100	102	90
1979	102	101	106	110	99	102	103	85
1980	100	97	105	114	98	106	102	84
1981	98	95	103	112	98	106	102	79
1982	99	97	103	107	94	105	104	71
1983	98	97	102	106	92	105	104	74
1984	100	98	110	108	97	108	99	74
1985	108	104	118	120	101	123	109	74
1986	114	110	125	132	104	129	105	84

Source: The Condition of Education, 1989.
         Vol.2: Postsecondary Education.
         (Washington: U.S. Dept. of Education,
         National Center for Education
         Statistics, 1989): p.110.

demonstrate the value of the assets we collect. Technology can help do that for us.

Most of us have or will soon have functioning online catalogs. On my own campus, when we brought up our OPAC, use of the local network increased dramatically—and administrators noticed. The fruit of MARC cataloging and conversion projects, the OPAC, opened a new window on our collections. Soon after bringing up the online catalog, we mounted as menu selections a variety of periodical indexes. Using the same search conventions as those in the OPAC, users could perform author, title, and keyword searches in those databases and switch quickly back to the OPAC to determine whether we own the title and, if we do, where it's located on campus. Since summary holdings are already online, the next step will be to note current issues. As logical extensions of this fairly minimal data, we also are exploring options for providing table of contents information and, beyond that, abstracts and fulltext for at least some titles. The object of these still fairly primitive technological innovations is to improve the product we are delivering to our patrons: to save them time, to broaden their information about the range of resources available for their use, to add value to the assets we are already accumulating by opening up their covers. This sort of exploitation of the possibilities of the new technologies, in my opinion, is crucial to the position of any library.

But this is only one example. Some other possibilities for more sharply defining the library's profile on campus are these:

- Providing lists to faculty of new books, journals, or materials in other formats recently added to the collection, sorted by subject. You could spin off this sort of product from either your acquisitions or cataloging system. You might also explore ways to identify titles that you would like to have acquired, but had to forego.[25]
- Taking responsibility for developing and maintaining a comprehensive, campus-wide bibliography of faculty publications, in machine-readable—and manipulable-format. Many campuses abandoned such bibliographies in times of cutbacks. You can readily imagine the various uses of such a record of "output." You could, for example, assess and compare the

relative intensity of research by discipline to the distribution of the collection budget.
— How many libraries have established and cultivated a formal information service link with their administrations? One way to maintain centrality is to provide services to those with the final say in budget allocation. Busy administrators are always in need of an apt anecdote or statistic or date. Assigning a competent, articulate person to the administration building information beat would be money well invested.
— Is the library seen as the central forum for debate on the many national and international issues that occupy so much of the talk in the coffeeshops and dormitories? Does the library sponsor speaker series and produce bibliographies on those topics? Why not? If not you, who?

Libraries that are part of very large campuses sometimes tend to view students as necessary evils. We hardly see their faces after a while; there are so many of them. At best, they are sources of cheap labor. Yet undergraduates, as any development officer will tell you, are a university's primary long-term source of donations and goodwill. Undergrads, after all, are a major reason we are in business, never mind that they become doctors and lawyers and elected officials. How much attention do we pay, as an institution, to our student hourly workers? Do we look for incentives to enhance their studies: access to micros, to database searching, to research help? As Edmund Burke observed, we are each bound by ties of affection to those "little platoons" that most closely touch our daily lives. If we do not forge those bonds out of decency, we ought to forge them at least out of self-interest.

How many of us have read a book like Tom Peters' THRIVING ON CHAOS?[26] Though focused primarily upon management in private sector enterprises, he concludes most chapters by identifying public sector parallels to his various suggestions. Do we, for example, have in place mechanisms for continually polling our users for suggestions for improvements? Do we, for example, as a routine part of planning regularly convene focus groups of students and faculty to assess services or test demand for new ones. And do we respond swiftly and visibly?

How aggressive are we in providing "information counseling" services? Quite apart from the fee-or-free debate (which is more accurately labeled fee-or-subsidized), students are paying a portion of their tuition for library services. How unjust that we are not more aggressive in teaching them to use the expensive access infrastructures we create for them. There is always more that could be done here.

The above is only a partial list of ideas for enhancing opportunities for increased internal funding. Every one of them would cost money, some of them a great deal. Yet, if we do not carve out of our already stretched budgets dollars for services that vividly demonstrate our centrality to the life of our campuses, we will not be able to hold even our present share of the pie.

The options for external funding are admittedly more limited. There certainly is money available for preservation-related activities. But apart from government and institutions, are there ways in which we might tap the private-sector? Can we, for example, identify enticements for commercial publishers? We are, after all, the locus of their markets. What might we exchange? For one thing, we have access to use patterns, market data that academic publishers often lack. In exchange for reduced or waived subscription fees and development costs, a library could track non-patron specific use data. Or perhaps, we could identify other, royalty-related projects. Such suggestions, certainly, will offend the sensibilities of some of my anti-market colleagues. But we ought not to apologize for seeking to maximize the resources available to our patrons. Nor are we obligated to adopt an excessively adversarial stance toward the sector that, after all, generates the wealth that buys our books and pays our salaries.

One of the managerial objectives for doing this sort of brainstorming, of course, should be to inculcate in our staffs a sense of urgency and to break the entitlement mentality that seems often to afflict those of us who work too long in public sector institutions; the mentality that insists that one ought to be supported because what one is doing is a self-evident good. As Gordon Tullock has observed, people who make their livings in such institutions tend to feel they should be rewarded for good intentions rather than for results.[27] What we must all realize is that, if we ever could, no longer can libraries expect their universities to automatically ante-up.

And perhaps by speaking to administrators in the result-oriented language of the manager, we will be in a position to credibly articulate and secure funding for those other ends we exist to serve; those sometimes hard-to-remember-in-the-rush-of-it-all ends, which, in the phrase of the great Swiss economist, Wilhelm Roepke, are "beyond supply and demand."[28] Oddly, the academy seems to continually need reminders that there are those other ends.

J. R. R. Tolkien, you know, was by profession a philologist. Read sometime his wonderful letters.[29] You'll see a harried, underpaid academic, continually swamped with lectures, grading, committee work, and professional obligations. His beloved *Lord of the Rings* was written in his spare time, over many years. His colleagues, apart from a small circle of like-minded friends, considered such tale-spinning as, frankly, trivial, self-indulgent, and beneath the dignity of a scholar. How ironic. One of the greatest works of imagination produced in this century, written in obscurity, arising not from the pressure to publish, but out of love and wonder, an enduring gift to generations that would have counted for nothing—or worse—had Tolkien been up for tenure review. Even Oxford can misjudge.

His book in its first few years was sometimes hard to get. Peter Beagle, in the foreword to a later paperback edition, mentions how he searched for four years before finally finding a copy—in the stacks of a research library. It was, it would seem, one of those titles at the margins. If, too, you want to read his now out-of-print letters, unless you can discover a copy in a secondhand shop somewhere, you'll find them only in a library. The world is full of such treasures that do not make many reading lists. A recent work by James Schall is such a one: *Another sort of learning*. Its marvelous subtitle says it all: "Selected contrary essays on how finally to acquire an education while still in college or anywhere else, containing some belated advice about how to employ your leisure time when ultimate questions remain perplexing in spite of your highest earned academic degree, together with sundry book lists nowhere else in captivity to be found."[30] One of the reasons, in fact, that Professor Schall wrote this little guidebook for the true student is that "real education and formal education may not be at all the same things."

We need to fight for funding in part so that we can continue to buy just these sorts of seemingly "out-of-scope" books. Because besides serving the immediately measurable utilitarian ends of a great research university—ends which certainly have value and social utility—we are also—let us say it out loud—the repositories of such documents. One of our key cultural ends is the acquisition and preservation of such odd, precious artifacts as the Tolkien letters and Schall essays or the little volume described on the invoice that is in the bin next to me as I write this, an updated list of political prisoners in the USSR. And not preservation as in a museum but as in a memory,[31] a memory in which our students—and maybe even some faculty—can seek after the highest things, the permanent things. That is not an easily quantifiable objective. But it is a real one. And among the myriad demands on the university purse, the provision of such a resource, open to all who are open to the search, is surely among the most basic, is, in fact, somewhere near the heart of what a liberal education is all about.

My own mentor once wrote an essay entitled, "Why Democratic Technocrats Need the Liberal Arts."[32] "The first and most important function of Liberal Arts education," he argues, "is to give amplitude and width to the human personality and to enable that personality to express itself fully, clearly, precisely, and gracefully"; to liberate and humanize, to educate the experts we train. Libraries are central to that mission, particularly in an age dominated by the machine. Because "(t)echnology," he points out, "divorced from a rational and human context is the great danger of our era and of our society . . . When the religious, humanistic, rationalist context of technology is . . . lost technology itself will have passed beyond the unwilling reach of mankind. The truth is that we can have the achievements of technology only so long as we will and wish beyond technology."

We should indeed seek to achieve efficiency in our internal processing operations. We should indeed seek to serve ever more effectively the increasingly feverish pace of research. We should indeed seek to exploit the full potential of the new communication technologies. But we should also seek opportunities to remind our distracted colleagues of that other role that the library serves as incarnate symbol of commitment to the liberating function of the academy.

REFERENCES

1. Twain, Mark. *Adventures of Tom Sawyer*. (New York: Modern Library, 1947): pp.54-55.
2. *Serials pricing newsletter*. (Chapel Hill, NC): no.16.
3. Geneen, Harold. *Managing*. (New York: Doubleday, 1984).
4. Lofquist, William. "Scholars vs. Publishers: Grounds for Divorce?" *Book research quarterly* (Winter 1988/89): p.54. *Book industry trends 1988*. (Scranton, PA: Book Industry Study Group, 1988): p.39. Okerson, Ann. *Of making many books there is no end*. Report on serial prices for the Association of Research Libraries. (Eastchester, NY: ARL, 1989): p.7.
5. Okerson, pp.13-14. "(I)n ARL university libraries over the period 1986-1988 . . . increased serials expenditures have directly affected the purchase of monographs. The additional funds to maintain serials collections have resulted in a decline of 15% in the number of monographs purchased."
6. Margaret Thatcher, television interview, 1980. *Macmillan dictionary of quotations*. (New York: Macmillan, 1989): p.373.
7. Munn, Robert F. "The Bottomless Pit, or the Academic Library as Viewed from the Administration Building." *College & Research Libraries* (November 1989): pp.635-37.
8. Goodstein, D.H. "Megatrends and Megabucks: the Economic Impact of Electronic Publication Technologies on the Professional Publisher and Information Consumer." *Electronic publishing: the new way to communicate*: Proceedings of the Symposium on Electronic Publishing, 5-7 November 1986, Luxembourg. (London: Kogan Page, 1987): p.27.
9. For a useful discussion, see Butler, Brett. "Scholarly Journals, Electronic Publishing, and Library Networks: From 1986 to 2000." *Serials review* (Summer/Fall 1986): pp.47-52. See also Piternick, Anne B. "Attempts to Find Alternatives to the Scientific Journal: A Brief Review." *Journal of academic librarianship* (November 1989): pp.260-66.
10. Private communication from Prof. Roman Szporluk, Director, Center for Russian and East European Studies, University of Michigan, to the author.
11. Veliotes, Nicholas A. "Copyright in the 1990s: A New Round of Challenges for American Publishers." *Book research quarterly* (Spring 1988): pp.3-11.
12. For a convenient description of the various networks, see LaQuey, Tracy. "Networks for Libraries." *Academic computing* (November 1989): pp.32ff.
13. Merriman, Greg and Walsh, Ami. "Evangelist of the Computer Age: Doug Van Houweling wants to make Ann Arbor a center for the information-based society of the future." *Ann Arbor Observer* (February 1990): p.31.

14. *Ibid.*, p.31.

15. Dijkstra, Jan Willem. "Factors in Setting Prices of Scientific Journals." *Book research quarterly* (summer 1988): p.19.

16. Merriman, p.32. Note, too, on the issue of increased cooperation between the public and private sectors that NSF recently authorized "(t)he creation of a new company to sell access to powerful computer-communications networks" which "may mark the beginning of the commercialization of the National Science Foundation's national research and education network." *Chronicle of higher education* (7 February 1990): p.A22.

17. *Ibid.*, p.33.

18. *Ibid.*, p.34. Some, by the way, may see in such increased cooperation between the public and the private sectors a threat to the independence of the university. Indeed, all money comes with strings. Of far greater concern, however, should be the increasingly heavy dependence of both public and private institutions on Federal and State appropriations and research funding. Public colleges and universities on average receive almost 80% of their revenues from that combination of sources; even private four-year institutions receive just under a quarter of their total funding from the state. (See U.S. Department of Education, National Center for Education Statistics. *Condition of education 1989*. Vol.2: *Postsecondary education*. (Washington, DC: DOE, 1989): pp.104-105.) A diversity of funding sources is, in the long term, a much safer policy if one is concerned about politicized pressure. And, given the present revenue configuration, the potential for unwarranted interference by corporations in the life of the academy pales before the real daily mischief of legislators and bureaucrats.

19. *Ibid.*, p.33.

20. *Condition of education*, vol.2: p.46. See also Noble, J. Kendrick. "Demographics and destiny." *Book research quarterly* (Spring 1989): pp.32-37; and Baensch, Robert E. "Consolidation in Publishing and Allied Industries." *Book research quarterly* (Winter 1988/89): pp.6-13.

21. *Condition of education*, vol.2: p.28.

22. Palca, Joseph. "Hard Times at NIH." *Science* (24 November 1989): p.988.

23. *Science* (16 January 1990): p.394.

24. *Condition of education*: Vol.2: p.110.

25. In the sciences, one could, for example, begin by working with the annual "new journals review" section of the September issue of *Nature*, noting those titles which would have been desirable to purchase but which the library could not afford. The issue of 28 September 1989 listed 127 new titles. The cost for one subscription to each would have been more than $20,000. One could also investigate ways in which, for example, one's approval plan vendors might be of help with lists of titles not selected.

26. Peters, Tom. *Thriving on chaos*: handbook for a management revolution. (New York: Knopf, 1987).

27. Tullock, Gordon. "Information Without Profit." *Papers on non-market decision making*. (Charlottesville, VA: Thomas Jefferson Center for Political

Economy, University of Virginia, 1966): Vol.1: pp.141-159. See also Buchanan, James M. and Devletoglou, Nicos E. *Academic in anarchy:* an economic diagnosis. (New York: Basic, 1970); and De Gennaro, Richard. "Technology & Access in the Enterprise Society." *Library journal* (1 October 1989): pp.40-43.

28. Roepke, Wilhelm. *The humane economy*: The social framework of the free market. (South Bend, IN: Gateway, 1960), especially Chapter 3.

29. Tolkien, J.R.R. *Letters of J.R.R. Tolkien*. Selected and edited by Humphrey Carpenter. (Boston: Houghton Mifflin, 1981).

30. Schall, James. V. *Another sort of learning*. (San Francisco: Ignatius Press, 1988).

31. For an example of academic "forgetfulness" in the understanding of modern political and intellectual movements, see Voegelin, Eric. *Science, politics & gnosticism*. (Chicago: Regnery Gateway, 1968); pp.3-7.

32. Tonsor, Stephen J. "Why Democratic Technocrats Need the Liberal Arts." *Freedom, order and the university*. (Malibu, CA: Pepperdine University Press, 1982): pp.19-30.

Balancing Collections, Balancing Budgets in Academic Libraries

Carolyn Bucknall

Library literature is larded with references to the "balanced collection." From the Library of Alexandria to the Library of Congress, we have aspired to attain the best in all fields of endeavor, seeking subject balance through comprehensive acquisitions. We have recognized virtue in a fair representation of opposing points of view, or of differing knowledge perspectives, as for example, the sciences and the humanities. We are concerned about equity among formats acquired and attempt to assign appropriate weights to serials and to monographs in any given discipline, and to print and nonprint formats. We have not historically hobbled ourselves with the limitations of present need, but have looked to the future as well. And we have looked backward, too, to acquire publications emanating from our scholarly past and present antecedents.

More recently we have made ritual farewells to Alexandria with some show of piety. We have solemnly reassured each other: "No library can any longer aspire to be self-sufficient." We have talked resource-sharing for so many years, we have convinced publishers that something illegal is taking place. If there is so much sharing of journal articles, they reason, why don't we get more copyright payments?

Now, beleaguered by financial pressures of unprecedented duration, we must balance our book budgets. This is a mandate. With balancing the resources budget imperative, is the ideal of "balancing" the collections still realistic? Or can that ideal of balance be going the way of multiple subscriptions to the same periodical title,

Carolyn Bucknall is Assistant Director for Collection Development at the University of Texas Libraries, Austin, TX.

© 1991 by The Haworth Press, Inc. All rights reserved.

arcane and leisurely original cataloging, and call numbers penned on spines in white ink with a round hand?

Perhaps we will view the period beginning in the mid-fifties and extending to 1985 as a kind of modern Golden Age of collection development. The period was delightful in many ways. The character of postwar publishing began to undergo really observable change in the mid-fifties as production burgeoned. Federal and state governments began to put unprecedented sums into higher education, a trend that William Axford characterized as "not unlike the 'whoopee' atmosphere of the boom towns on the mining frontier during the last half of the nineteenth century."[1] Funding was abundant. Through the emphasis on research in higher education, academic libraries were enjoying unparalleled acquisitions budgets.

When Richard Abel arrived as the right man at the right time, the stage was set for dramatic changes. Traditional faculty control of book selection was inadequate for spending large sums, especially in a context of accelerated publishing worldwide. Approval plans developed by Abel and others were a means for effecting changes that held much appeal for librarians. For with the introduction of approval plans faculty responsibility for selection was broken. Bibliographers who were also subject specialists were installed to monitor the plans and perform other selection duties. Lacking extended field experience and a well defined conceptual framework for collecting decisions, these pioneers were quick to recognize a serious deficiency. What was needed was a systematic, rationalized approach to collection building by librarians. When ultimately implemented, this basic framework included a number of elements that have become so familiar to all of us: selection by library bibliographers, faculty liaison by bibliographers, the formulation of collection development policies, collection management and evaluation programs, and so on.

As in prior Golden Ages the selection structure was built on two premises: (1) Libraries exist to further the goals of their parent institutions, and (2) Libraries exist to serve present and future institutional needs.

These articles of faith have permeated our current collection development policies, many of which had roots in the 70s. Typically policy statements on each discipline still begin with a statement of purpose (the support of specified academic programs) and proceed to explain that the collection thus developed is to support current *and future* scholarship on the subject. The two do pull in opposite directions noted Robert Stueart, saying: "Disagreement still persists as to the desirability of 'comprehensiveness' over that of recognized 'need':[2]

> Some writers maintain that those conditions are mutually exclusive. For example, Poole, writing about public libraries over a hundred years ago, declared that to meet 'the varied wants of readers there must be on the shelves of the library books which persons of culture never read', although they may want to do so at some future time.[3]

Contradictory or not, Golden Age gospel was preached with missionary zeal. With the distancing of time we may come to recognize that some tenets regarded as "truths" were simply good ideas for the times — that is, relative "truths." The concept of "collection balance" may be one of these ideas.

Conventional collection development wisdom has held that a research library worthy of the name must acquire as comprehensively as possible from the world's total academically relevant current book production. The early measure of approval plan effectiveness, for instance, was not in the number of *needed* volumes received, but in the *comprehensiveness* of the plan. These premises have been at least modified, if not negated, by the present economic climate in higher education.

Since the ideal of collection comprehensiveness, or balance, is justifiable only in terms of future rather than present need, we are reduced to asking a most simplistic question: Where do we draw the line between present and future academic needs? *Where* in all probability will be much closer to needs for today and considerably short of needs for the next hundred years. Generally we will be buying books to suit present institutional needs and those predicated on needs for the next year or the next decade, according to the vision and financial resources of the parent institution. The trend for those who have not yet arrived at this point is definitely toward a core of immediately usable, locally-needed materials.

The term "balance" is also applied to the desired budget relationship between monographs and serials. Homely formulas have been invoked to show that the ratio of serials to monographs should be under 50 percent in 1970, but 60 percent in 1980.[4] As the largest and most rapidly growing budget cost center, serials are a logical target for quick budget reduction. Moreover, the necessity for serial cancellations, because of the great amount of publicity given to the cost of scholarly journals and because of our own local public education efforts, is widely recognized and accepted. But no universal standard can tell us the correct budget portion to be applied to serial subscriptions, even on a subject basis. Ultimately, a library must look to its own goals and evaluate the effectiveness with which they are being met.

Indeed, comparing the serials held by one library to those held by another proves very little. About the only kind of generalized core list of serials that makes sense is a compilation of basic titles—a kind of lowest common denominator. Beyond that level, journal selection must be guided by local programs. Going a step further and making actual use the criterion for an institution-specific list of core journals is certainly feasible technically, though we might have difficulty in measuring uncharged uses. Obviously our libraries are in varying stages of financial need. For some the idea of paring serials to those that are actually used, say at least once a year, is still unthinkable. For other libraries that point has already been reached, even transcended.

Ironically, the move toward serials divestment comes at a time when even the user of small libraries may encounter numerous electronic references to journals that were not formerly accessible via printed indexes. In actual cancellation projects, once duplicate subscriptions are largely eliminated, the focus has been on little used (and hopefully expensive) research titles. These were acquired in many instances because they were perceived as the hallmark of a respectable research program. If usage does not justify such subscriptions, we are paying a heavy price for prestige.

How are we to provide our scholars with articles from journals to which we do not subscribe? For years publishers have listened to librarians talk about resource sharing and have concluded that they are missing out on a sizeable chunk of the action. Despite our talk, however, very little was done on a large scale except among institutions that are in close geographical proximity. More intense activity was impeded by the lack of a viable means of document delivery.

Now expedited document delivery from commercial services and from other libraries *via* fax has become commonplace for a fee. Fax equipment is improving. More libraries are undertaking to serve others on a contractual basis. Receiving libraries are making arrangements for paying copyright fees just as do commercial suppliers. As publisher income from these sources begins to show recognizable increases, a message is delivered: Growing numbers of libraries are not subscribing to this journal, but they are willing to pay for needed articles, many of them forwarded by expedited facsimile transmission. A significant level of such messages can constitute a market force that will encourage the expansion of electronic journal publishing.

A group of research libraries has become concerned about what will happen to all the worthwhile journals that nobody will consider core to local programs, should paring actually be broadly implemented. In particular, the fear had grown that the unanimously cancelled title would cease to exist or become totally unavailable in North America. To address this eventuality, a generalized "core" list that includes foreign languages and titles of a supplementary or peripheral nature has been developed for several disciplines. Each participant will volunteer to retain lesser-held titles from these lists. This effort at coordinated collection development may succeed in at least one of its purposes, but the expense is not negligible since the four lists so far developed were over two years in the making.

A more promising line of cooperation at this level is offered by the Center for Research Libraries, whose entire serials subscription program is limited to lesser-held titles. As member libraries gain the capacity to load tapes of the Center's cataloging records into local online catalogs, connections are set in place to take full advantage of the Center's collections, including many of those serial holdings the local institution is likely to have eliminated.

In sum, here are some of the strategies for managing serials costs and striking what is a locally desirable balance between serials and monographs: continuing serials review and cancellations based on use, and emphasis on alternate sources for journal articles including cooperative ventures such as local consortia and the Center for Research Libraries.

Another aspect of managing serials costs relates to the balance between the sciences and the humanities. Again, forming a generalized optimum ratio between dollars spent on sciences and dollars spent on humanities serials is not feasible. Judging from evolving priorities, the sciences are still primarily journal-dependent. However, monographs, especially handbooks, treatises, and conference proceedings, are also necessary to the sciences and expensive as well. Research and instruction in the humanities, while needing a much less costly journals base than in the sciences, also requires broad monographic support in as much depth as the institution can muster. History of science aside, scientific monographs will be used for a few years and relegated to storage or withdrawn. But a large percentage of monographs in the humanities, purchased to answer present needs, will continue to be useful indefinitely or until they are finally worn out. The social sciences seem to fall somewhere between these two models.

Before the price of serials (and scientific serials in particular) skyrocketed, it was convenient to think of serials expenditures as being weighted in favor of the sciences, while approval plan expenditures were weighted in favor of the humanities, with social sciences being maintained well in both. Now we are growing uneasy with the distribution of funding. Not only do the sciences claim a lion's share of serials expenditures, but prices for scientific monographs are growing as well. Excluding reference works, costs of single-volume proceedings and treatises are more often being seen in the $300-$500 range.

What we would like to maintain in our budget allocations for the broad areas of learning and between the various disciplines is an equity principle that I call the "pain factor." Once appropriate funding levels are ascertained, make necessary cuts in such a manner that the pain is equally felt. Maintaining this kind of balance is a very tough judgement call. While in the best of cases our budget allocation decisions are buttressed by an array of statistical and programmatic information, in the final analysis the allocation process is an art, not a science.

Cost control strategies will also involve reconsideration of approval plans. Profiles for domestic approval plans are increasingly focused on specific institutional programs. In reappraisals based on current need and anticipated present use, foreign approval plans are typically the first targets for reduction or elimination. The curtailment of scientific monographic acquisitions is another possible measure suggested by the foregoing.

Approval plans are not the only gathering plans in need of review. The library may want to consider more blanket orders with publishers, comprehensive subscriptions, and depository arrangements as ways to automatically acquire the relevant or total output of publishers recognized as core within the local context. Standing orders for monographic series can also be reviewed from this perspective. In all these acquisitions methods the receipt of current titles quickly upon publication is of real consequence, both to serve library users well and to take advantage of the brief windows of acquisitions opportunity characteristic of the more limited press runs in today's publishing.

Mass purchasing arrangements also reduce staff time spent in selection, order placement, receiving and payment, and other processing. Over the years, as gathering plans have proved effective acquisitions tools, acquisitions staff have been freed for other activities. During the same period selectors' time constraints have grown with the introduction of new technologies and information services. More focused gathering plans will likely lead to more title-by-title orders. In typical circumstances purchasing power (and therefore conventional order placement) for individual libraries has already been so reduced that existing staff can be expected to absorb consequent additional work. However, if existing approval plans are dissolved so that all acquisitions are obtained through conventional orders, the disparity between manpower and workload could be significant and a new problem created while an old one was being solved. Comparative analysis of the numbers of volumes received by the various methods over the last several years will help to predict likely staff impacts for the planned acquisitions strategy.

The library selection plan is emerging as a popular alternative to full-fledged approval plans. When selection by a vendor is not judged to be satisfactory for whatever reason, some libraries have elected to convert the arrangement into a library selection plan based usually on vendor-supplied forms, but also on marked copies of national bibliographies or other simplified order mechanisms. Because of reduced processing costs, these libraries still prefer a somewhat complicated approval plan offshoot over conventional title-by-title ordering. Certainly stricter financial controls are possible with this variation. Dana Alessi suggests that the transformation of paper selection forms into tapes that match the library profile may generate a new kind of library selection plan for current books. Titles would be locally selected from the tapes, orders generated through the local system, and the on-order record placed in appropriate local databases.[5]

If gathering plans are really cost effective, and I think they are, libraries (and vendors) will take advantage of this highly desirable feature by developing other hybrids as well. Further, potential for change as a result of electronic developments is great. In the final analysis whatever mix of mass purchasing and conventional ordering is chosen must be determined by local collection development goals within the context of local funding and staff availability.

Gathering plans are but one component in an acquisitions strategy that also includes serial subscriptions and conventional order placement for current and retrospective monographs. To complete our consideration of collection balance we must look more carefully at foreign and retrospective acquisitions, electronic resources, and non-print media.

Jeffrey Gardner's comments at this conference about the effects of reduced foreign purchases on the national well-being are certainly worthy of study by the Association of Research Libraries and of possible concerted action. The form that such action might take remains to be seen. Some have suggested that thought be given to a revival of the Farmington Plan or a similar scheme of cooperative foreign acquisitions in order to make sure that important current foreign titles will reside in a North American library. Like the research libraries project that has devoted considerable effort to fairly comprehensive listings of journals earmarked for rescue, this particular solution appears wide of the mark.

The problem with such schemes is: (1) they assume that the higher education, library, and publishing environments will continue pretty much as they have in the past, (2) they focus on future, not present need, (3) they reflect a saviour outlook that may bear little relationship to institutional goals. Possibly such efforts result from the balanced, comprehensive collection ideal so long embedded in our collection building canons.

I am told that when problem solving Europeans seek to ameliorate undesired conditions while Americans try to eradicate them. The shower of Utopian projects coming out of the profession at this time (to which I will add transforming the library into a journals publisher, and overturning the system of faculty promotion and tenure) may also be reflective of this same "all or nothing" American attitude.

Considering the rapidity of momentous changes occurring in the 80s, there is scant reason to suppose that forces in this very dynamic library and information environment will suddenly grind to a halt. Extensive communications networks have been laid and are being laid; we are beginning to consult each other's online catalogs, themselves being rapidly enhanced to include a variety of additional electronic information; document delivery has taken a quantum leap forward with improved fax equipment, the organization of the world of publishing has been dramatically altered with mergers, takeovers and buyouts; print runs have been much reduced; and preservation has become an enormous library cost center, particularly in research libraries.

New technologies have certainly affected our acquisitions budgets, particularly in the case of CD-ROM serial titles. New generations of students brought up on television have brought increased audiovisual emphasis to instruction. The value of a photograph as a research tool is recognized as never before, and video images are being placed on laser disks. We are providing all of these and more, along with the machines required to access them. With some of these formats we do a better job than with others. How many CD-ROMs should we buy? As many as we can afford once selection criteria are met. What we can afford, of course, is again a function of local priorities. As a general strategy most of us are using our "materials" budgets for traditional resources and for the acquisition of new technologies, new formats as they appear. We then strive to obtain a representative sampling of those that are useful.

If we are not to conduct business as usual, the pre-1985 collecting levels in our collection development policies will have to be rolled back. We have said all along that these policies are intended to be flexible, are subject to continuing review and revision. And so they are. But such revisions to date have been relatively minor or have related to changes in academic programs. To my knowledge no one has undertaken a massive scaling down of written policies that will in effect reduce depth across the board. My guess, however, is that quite a bit of downscaling has already taken place, foreign and retrospective acquisitions being an obvious case in point. These changes are simply not reflected in the policies. Why?

We know that past economic downturns, in terms of library purchasing power, have been cyclical. We have adopted short-term acquisitions and budget strategies and hoped that in the next fiscal year, or the next biennium, funding would improve. Meanwhile, we have educated our constituencies as to the need for serials cancellations, reduced foreign approval plans, meager retrospective purchasing, and generally reduced monographic acquisitions.

So part of our reluctance to change is experience. Historically funding has improved after downturns. Another part of our reluctance has to do with letting go of old tenets that may still be valuable. Ellsworth Mason at a 1975 conference, "Touching Bottom in the Bottomless Pit," contended that "bigger *is* better [emphasis mine]. In our enthusiasm for new directions in librarianship, we are likely to get the idea that things we do for the sake of economy are good in themselves, but they are not necessarily so."[6] We know we were building great libraries in the old way. We wonder whether the development of great libraries is possible in a financial environment that is significantly curtailed. Can we now cooperate in the intellectual dismantling of the carefully crafted collection development theories, goals, and policies in which we all have such heavy, personal and institutional investment?

The following comments assume that the library director has already established excellent relations with the University administration, that the library's somewhat shaky situation is fully understood, and the library is receiving its fair share of University funding—itself much reduced in purchasing power compared to pre-1985 days.

We are at the end of an era. I am convinced that the current economic climate for higher education will continue indefinitely.

Short term measures growing out of old philosophies are simply not adequate to the task of restructuring our budgets. What is required is nothing short of a reordering of priorities, including the confrontation of sacred cows. Not just librarians' sacred cows, but a whole collection of the critters. These can take the form of special collections, area studies, undergraduate libraries, media centers, pet programs of X, Y, or Z. We must analyze the changing roles of our various sacred cows, their costs, their relation to academic programs, and their political support. Because the issue of limited resources is really broader than collections and indeed encompasses the entire library, we will ultimately have to cast dispassionate and appraising eyes on the entire array of library services offered. We need to develop political strategies that set the stage for a reordering of priorities.

If one's library is fortunate enough to be attached to an institution that has actually reordered academic priorities, following that lead may be painful, but the signposts at least are evident. Without such activity in one's institution, political roads are rocky and perilous. The first step is making sure there is universal recognition that cuts in library acquisitions must be made. "Business as usual" expenditures which have emphasized some cost centers at the expense of others are points of departure for a possible reordering of priorities. Analysis of the costs of past acquisitions emphases is a way to document the need for correction. As noted by Murray Martin, "Items to look for include changes in total budget, changes in relationships between the various parts, and patterns of expenditure. The latter, in particular, should be compared with such matters as numbers of items purchased." Variations, he observes, may suggest "that item prices have forced a redistribution of [purchasing] effort."[7]

This phenomenon, of course, has been widely observed as increased serial costs have displaced a significant portion of monographic acquisitions. The same technique can also reveal growth in book production or fluctuation in item prices by country, with attendant cost increments. The approach is particularly valuable, along with appropriate subject analysis, in assessing the *de facto* priorities accorded the various country-based approval plans in a single institution. Historical analyses in turn should be compared to the goals and objectives of the collection development program as stated in the collection development policies.

To summarize, in this extended period of reduced purchasing power with no end in sight libraries are perceiving the need for more longer term remedies. In addition to the various tools we have always had at our disposal—acquisitions strategies, budgetary strategies, resource sharing strategies, and document delivery strategies—we will need to change the way we think about collection development. This is an analytical process that will take place over time and will be influenced by powerful forces in our present and future environments. It is not too early to begin to meet with interested faculty and bibliographers to discuss strategies and the larger need for a reordering of priorities. We will undoubtedly be looking at a downgrading of the collection development policy across the board. We will be making extensive financial analyses, past and present, of the costs and volumes received through the various acquisitions methods. And we will begin preparation of plans for reordered priorities, with all of the attendant forums and discussions that implies.

I would like to turn for a moment to the first gathering programs of which I spoke earlier. One of the most-cited reasons for instituting approval plans back in the 60s was to improve on faculty-based collection development. Those titles *not* selected by faculty included: (1) titles outside the faculty member's own (sometimes narrowly construed) area of interest, (2) titles needed by students but not by faculty, and (3) titles in new or emerging fields not yet incorporated into the academic programs. Perhaps most significant, only a small percentage of faculty were actively involved in book selection. Frequently selections not only failed to represent student interests, but also failed to represent interests of other colleagues. (A new generation of faculty later appeared not to be particularly interested in the challenges of collection development.)

This leads to a list of strategies I do not want to use, presuming a continuation of current environmental conditions. I do not want to:

1. return to reliance on faculty selection as a by-product of need-oriented, demand-driven acquisitions.
2. become a journal publisher because errant commercial publishers need good competition
3. develop a generalized "core" journals list by discipline, including all basic journals, all those essential for limited study

and research, and all that appear "solid" yet peripheral to typical extended research programs
4. resurrect the Farmington Plan
5. reform the academic system of promotion and tenure in order to improve scholarly journals

And finally, in terms of my own institution which has a total enrollment of 50,000, with 36,000 undergraduates, I do not want to cancel domestic approval plan.

To return to the question posed at the beginning of this talk — Is the ideal of maintaining a balanced collection realistic? It should be apparent by now that I believe this ideal is fast losing ground. We already have collections in which the "balance" is disappearing — not necessarily a bad thing in itself. We will have more. We will have gaps in subject coverage. We will have serial files terminated in mid-course.

Obviously these are trying times. Our institutional woes have roots in national economic policy that we as librarians cannot eradicate. It appears we must opt for a rather anti-heroic stance: amelioration of our own institutional problems.

I spoke of the end of an age. Of course lines of historical demarcation occur only in retrospect. In reality we are working in a dual mode, with one foot in the past and one in the future. We know where we have been, but where we are going is still a matter of some speculation in a climate of intensive change. Joan Wadlow, in her introductory remarks to this conference spoke truly when she said that libraries are windows to the future. Meanwhile we must respond to our present challenges with as much grace, intelligence, forethought, imagination, and — yes, patience — that we can muster.

NOTES

1. H. William Axford, "Approval Plans: An Historical Overview and an Assessment of Future Value," in *Shaping Library Collections for the 1980s*, ed. Peter Spyers-Duran and Thomas Mann, Jr. (Phoenix, Ariz.: Oryx Press, 1980), p. 19.

2. Robert D. Stueart in "Introduction" to *Collection Development in Libraries: A Treatise*, ed. Robert D. Stueart and George B. Miller, Jr. (Greenwich, Conn.: JAI, 1980), p. xviii.

3. Stueart, "Introduction" p. xvii.

4. Murray Martin, "The Allocation of Money within the Book Budget," in *Collection Development in Libraries: A Treatise,* ed. Robert D. Stueart and George B. Miller, Jr. (Greenwich, Conn.: JAI Press, 1980), p. 59.

5. Dana Alessi, "Coping with Library Needs: The Approval Vendor's Response/Responsibility," in *Issues in Acquisitions: Programs and Evaluations,* ed. Sul H. Lee (Ann Arbor: Pierian Press, 1984), p. 106.

6. Ellsworth Mason, "Opportunities and Obstacles: A Panel Discussion," in Farewell to Alexandria: *Solutions to Space, Growth, and Performance Problems in Libraries,* ed. Daniel Gore. (Westport, Conn.: Greenwood Press, 1976), p. 151.

7. Martin, "Allocation of Money," p. 48

For Product Safety Concerns and Information please contact our EU
representative GPSR@taylorandfrancis.com
Taylor & Francis Verlag GmbH, Kaufingerstraße 24, 80331 München, Germany

www.ingramcontent.com/pod-product-compliance
Lightning Source LLC
Chambersburg PA
CBHW052130300426
44116CB00010B/1847